C is for CAT

An easy guide to veterinary care for cats

Dr. Terrie Sizemore DVM

This is a work of non-fiction.
Text and Illustrations copyrighted
by Terrie Sizemore, DVM, RN ©2016

Library of Congress Control Number: 2016919897

All rights reserved. No part of this book may be
reproduced, transmitted, or stored in an information retrieval
system in any form or by any means,
graphic, electronic, or mechanical without prior written
permission from the author.

First Edition 2016

Printed in the United States of America
A 2 Z Press LLC
PO Box 582
Deleon Springs, FL 32130
bestlittleonlinebookstore.com
bestlittleonlinebookstore@gmailcom
386-681-7402

ISBN: 978-1-946908-98-8

Dedication

This book is dedicated in
loving memory
of my beloved grandfather,
Alexander Balcziunas.

TABLE OF CONTENTS

Preface ....**v**
Introduction...**vi**
Chapter 1: Cats - the Most Popular Pet in America.......**1**
Chapter 2: Getting Started **9**
Supplies 13
Setting up the House 20
Kitty Proofing the house 21
Picking a Veterinarian..24
Chapter 3: Vaccines **27**
The major preventable diseases 28
Transmission of germs...29
The vaccine controversy 32
Why vaccinate 34
Rhinotracheitis 36
Calicivirus..40
Panleukopenia..42
Leukemia..45
Chlamydia..49
FIP- feline infectious peritonitis 52
FIV- feline immunodeficiency virus....................................55
Rabies 57
Bordetella.............:...63
Toxoplasmosis 66
Special needs for kittens 72
Adverse reactions to vaccines..74
Chapter 4: Spaying and neutering **77**
Reasons to spay..82
Reasons to neuter 83
When to spay and neuter..84
Complications of spaying and neutering.............................86
Minimize complications of spaying and neutering.............87
Chapter 5: What your cat is expecting **89**
Getting Pregnant 90
Yes! We're pregnant...91
Benefits of x-rays when pregnant 92
Being prepared 94
Stage 1 of kitten delivery 96
Stage 2 of kitten delivery 97

Stage 3 of kitten delivery 98
When to worry 101
What to do..102
How old do you think your kitten is?...............................105
Bottle feeding...106
Medications safe for use in pregnant cats 109
Medications not safe for use in pregnant cats.................110
Chapter 6: Dental care 113
Tooth eruption...114
Stages of tartar buildup 116
Signs and symptoms cats need dental care 120
Reasons for dental care 121
Preventative care for dental needs 122
Brushing your pet's teeth 124
Definitions about dental needs of cats 125
Chapter 7: Nutrition 127
Stages of development..128
Types of diets..130
Weight management diets...132
Goals for weight management 136
Benefits of lower calorie foods.......................................138
Treats..139
Chapter 8: Arthritis...141
Types of Arthritis 142
Predisposing factors for arthritis.....................................143
Signs of arthritis..146
Diagnosis of arthritis...152
Goals for pet owners...153
Treatment for arthritis...154
Chapter 9: Poisons 161
Signs of poisoning...162
Most common poisonings in cats....................................163
What to do if a pet is poisoned..169
Chapter 10: Training..171
Common behavior issues in cats.....................................178
How to socialize your cats 183
Chapter 11: Diagnostic Testing 185
Common tests recommended..186
Fecal tests..187
Common intestinal worms in cats...................................188

Roundworms 191
Hookworms 192
Tapeworms 194
Coccidia 197
Bloodwork 198
Facts about blood 200
Complete blood counts 201
Chemistry 202
Electrolytes 204
Pancreas tests 205
Thyroid tests 206
BUN and creatinine 209
Diabetic testing 211
Heartworm disease in cats 213
Leukemia/Immunodeficiency/Heartworm testing 217
Hepatic Lipidosis 218
X-rays 222
Ultrasound 223
Advanced imaging 224
Skin testing 225
Skin scraping 228
Notoedric mange 229
Fleas 230
Cultures 231
Ringworm 232
Fungal cultures 233
Feline acne 234
Urine exams 235
Disorders of the urinary system 236
Urine testing 237
Signs of ear disorders 239
Ear exams 240
Ear care 241
Ear mites 242
Signs of eye disorders 243
Eye exam 245
Staining tests for the eye 246
Tear testing for the eye 247
Pressure testing for the eye 248
Cat scratch fever 249

Hairballs 251
Chapter 12: Miscellaneous 255
Lost pets 256
Microchipping 257
Emergencies 258
What to do in an emergency 259
Checking temperature, heart rate, and breathing rate 260
First aid kits 263
Doing your own pet exam 264
Senior pets 271
Brushing 277
Bathing 278
Cat ages 279

PREFACE

I have been a busy veterinarian for many years and have had the unique experience of meeting people from many backgrounds in my varied practice.

I have observed that pet owners would like to learn, know, feel confident, and understand more about pet care for the cats they love and engage with everyday.

It is my intent to create a book that simplifies technical medical information so that cat owners and readers become informed without being overwhelmed. I hope to eliminate the frustration some owners face and encourage owners and readers to continue their quest for knowledge. I am convinced informed owners make better owners and will make better decisions for their pets.

It is also my hope that every owner and reader not only enjoys the basic and easy to understand information in this book but that, after reading it, they can, with confidence, seek great care for their pets.

This book is written to provide owners with basic general information regarding cat needs and care.

This work is not intended to be a substitute for veterinary care. No one can learn the professional discipline of being a veterinarian from a book. You, as the reader, will quickly realize many disorders overlap in signs and symptoms and there is caution to not overlook serious illness as much as not to mistake simple, uncomplicated disorders for more serious illness.

Please seek veterinary care for your pet as needed. Some situations encountered with your beloved pets require immediate attention.

Enjoy this book! Terrie Sizemore DVM

INTRODUCTION

Both dogs and cats are close companions, however, every cat owner knows that to know and own a cat is to love a cat.

Every day in my chosen professions, I make technical medical information understandable to my clients and patients.

Cats have many roles in the lives of people, however most are close companions to families, individuals and children. They are company for their owners as well as make childhood a most memorable time.

I have always said, 'the people who do not like cats, do not know cats.' Each has its own distinct personality and adds so much to owners' lives. Keeping them healthy and with their owners and families is what I do every day.

"C is For Cat" provides basic knowledge for every cat owner. The subjects range from vaccines for major preventable diseases in cats to reasons for spaying and neutering, what to expect when our cats are expecting, arthritis, dental care, emergency care, performing a physical exam, geriatric concerns, nutritional care for cats emphasizing overweight management, poisonous substances to cats, and a very brief chapter on behavioral issues.

Chapter 1
CATS ARE

THE MOST POPULAR PET IN AMERICA

At the creation of this book, the total number of 'households' owning dogs outnumber the total number of 'households' owning cats, however, the total number of cats as pets outnumbers the total number of dogs. And…..

…no matter if you selected a special breed of kitten……
… like this beautiful Siamese…

… or a Burmese, Himalayan, Turkish Angora, Russian Blue….

Persian…..

Tonkinese, British Shorthair, Sphynx, American Bobtail, Ragdoll, Maine Coon……

Balinese, Havana Brown, Peter Bald, Manx, Ragamuffin……
Bengal…..

Devon Rex, Cornish Rex, Abyssinian, Somali, Turkish Van…..
Or any of the other numerous breeds of cats….

Or, decided to adopt from one of the many shelters around town....

Or, like me…you picked what is called a plain old alley cat……

It is important to remember that we remember…..

> Just like the rest of the family, our cats need the proper nutrition, exercise, love, and medical care.

Veterinarians are also committed to the best care for your pet and are certain you want to understand care recommendations so you as cat owners can make great choices for your furred (and sometimes not furred) friends.

Chapter 2
Getting Started

When bringing our treasures home... some considerations are…...

Some cats and kittens come into our homes as if they have owned the house all along- immediately they are in and active and all around- we know these kind….

…. however, though bringing some cats home is exciting for us…

….it may be frightening for cats or kittens – especially when there are other pets in the home.
I recommend giving a new arrival somewhere to hide for a while - keeping them safe from being lost under furniture and preventing any escape outdoors through windows or open doors.

When given time to adjust, kittens may be shy at first, but ….

…..they warm up quickly and …

….suddenly! You have your hands full!

Be aware….

It may take some time for everyone to get along. Some cats adjust quickly to other pets in the home and others may take longer. Some cats never get quite adjusted to others.

Supplies

When kitty shopping…..

….. items that may come in handy are….

- food and treats
- carriers
- ceramic or stainless steel bowls
- collars that are breakaway – so cats can be freed if their collars are caught while jumping
- harnesses
- ID tags with your name and phone number
- brushes, combs and cat shampoo
- and …..

…. don't forget the toys!

Cats are very playful.

Many owners no longer consider declawing cats and in some states it is not permitted, so…..

…scratching posts may come in handy …… to avoid…….

….. this little mishap.

In addition to keeping the nails clipped, another option to avoid scratching furniture and drapes is…..

Soft paws.

These nail covers come in all colors, are easy to glue to the claws (this can also be done at your veterinarian's office) …. and….. come in various sizes.

And after playing, cats' next favorite activity is sleeping,

Cats and kittens sleep anywhere, but you can provide blankets, hammocks, boxes, beds, or other items to help them be comfortable.

Setting up the house

Setting up is another step in preparing for the new arrival….

Arranging the house includes deciding:
- how many litter boxes are needed
- where to put the boxes- so cats have easy access and dogs do not
- where to place cat food and toys and things – especially with other pets in the home or homes with multiple cats

Kitten-Proofing the Home

Don't forget to kitten-proof the house by remembering to:

1. Cover the electrical cords. Some owners cover them with the cardboard center of the toilet paper roll while others use throw rugs to cover cords or tape cords to the floor, some unplug the home to prevent kitten injury or loss
2. Store breakable and precious items where playful kittens cannot damage them
3. Keep all clothing, nylons, and strings out of the pet's reach – if swallowed, these can get stuck in the intestines of a cat or kitten and require surgery to be removed
4. Close windows and make certain screens are secured to prevent a new, possibly frightened pet from escaping the home while they are adjusting to their new home and neighborhood
5. Store poisonous cleaning chemicals out of reach of cats and kittens- store them behind doors with child proof

latches. – pesticides, laundry detergents, bleach, paint thinners, antifreeze, disinfectants, tub and tile cleaners, rodent chemicals and more

(Continued Kitten Proofing the Home)

6. Keep pets away from high decks or upper porches where they may fall from
7. Keep the toilet seats down to prevent accidents
8. Remove poisonous plants from your home- or mount them too high for a cat or kitten to reach
9. Keep all sewing supplies safely tucked away- cats love to play with string or rubber bands or ribbon or garland and can swallow string and needles easily
10. Store plastic bags so kittens cannot play inside them – this may be a hazard
11. Close dressers drawers and closets- cats like to sleep in dark spaces and may be trapped
12. Keep dryers and washers, microwaves and dishwashers closed- check before use
13. Putting out lit candles when cats or kittens are not being observed
14. Be careful with hot irons- cats may topple them over
15. Keep small toys with breakable parts away from cats
16. Keep cats away from car chemicals –the most dangerous chemical is antifreeze
17. Keep cooler lids closed – cats have been trapped inside accidentally
18. Keep breakable ornaments and decorations out of reach

And always remind children at home and visiting to be kind and gentle with the pets.

Last but not least:

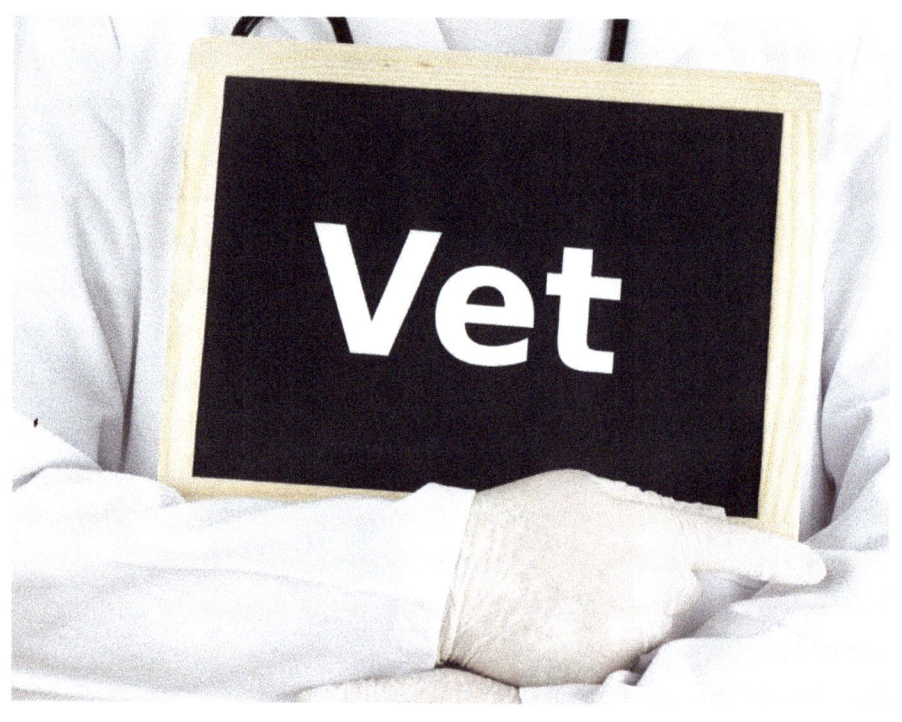

... don't forget to pick a veterinarian!

PICKING A VETERINARIAN

WHAT TO CONSIDER WHEN CHOOSING YOUR PET'S DOCTOR

Some clinics provide
- general service
- some are exclusive or mixed for horses
- some service farm animals
- some are 'cats only'
- some treat birds, fish, reptiles, and exotics

Other clinics have specialists for advanced care for:
- surgical needs
- skin diseases
- bone care
- eye/ear/neurological issues
- and other specialty concerns

NOW THAT WE HAVE WELCOMED OUR CATS, SOME BASIC TOPICS OF PET CARE INCLUDED IN THIS BOOK ARE:

- vaccines
- spaying and neutering
- what to expect when your cat is expecting
- dental care (teeth)
- nutrition
- arthritis in cats
- pet poisons
- training and behavior
- frequently recommended testing
- pet parasites
- fleas
- senior pets
- comparing cat to human ages
- finding lost pets
- emergency care
- cat exams at home
- bathing cats
- and more!

Chapter 3
Vaccines and Disease

Many years ago, scientists studied germs and disease. No one believed very small, microscopic 'things'—AKA germs—could enter a person's or pet's body and cause disease.

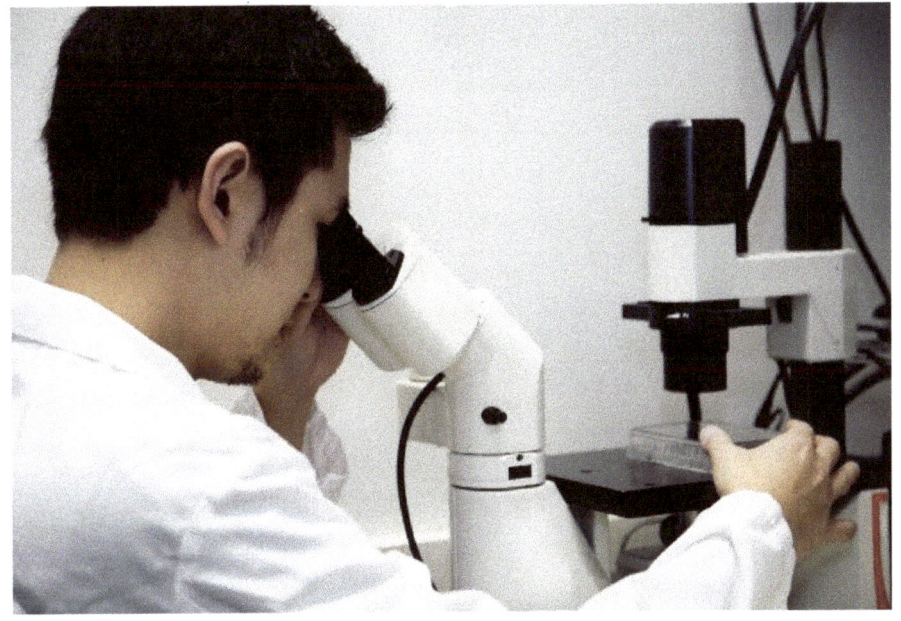

"GERMS" include:
- bacteria
- viruses
- fungi—which includes yeast and molds

THE MAJOR PREVENTABLE DISEASES

Panleukopenia –distemper

Calicivirus

Chlamydia

Infectious Peritonitis

Rabies

Rhinotracheitis

Toxoplasmosis

Bordetella

Leukemia   Immunodeficiency virus

Today more is known about germs and disease. Microscopic organisms do indeed cause diseases that affect our cats.

TRANSMISSION OF GERMS

Cats encounter infectious organisms—GERMS—that cause all the following diseases by:

- touch—direct contact from cat to cat
- mother cats transferring disease to their babies – either through the placenta when pregnant, through milk when nursing, or direct contact after birth
- exposure to fecal material, (AKA poop)
- saliva of infected cats
- wildlife—such as raccoons, skunks, coyotes and more
- fleas, mosquitoes and ticks
- rodents
- exposure to water—puddles, lakes, and other waterways contaminated with disease-causing germs
- "fomites"—objects that carry germs: like boots, pants legs, backpacks, and other physical objects

Scientists created vaccines to protect cats from disease.

When well cats are vaccinated, they make protective proteins called antibodies against the diseases they are vaccinated for. This protection allows them to fight infection if exposed to real germs.

Goals when vaccinating are:

- pets will not become ill,
- or, the illness will be less severe

THE VACCINE CONTROVERSY

There has been much controversy over vaccines:

- Will vaccines hurt my cat?
- What vaccines should I give?
- How often should I vaccinate?
- How many vaccines should I give at one time?
- Are they really necessary

Despite the controversy over vaccinating, and while it is true there are minimal risks to vaccinating cats…..

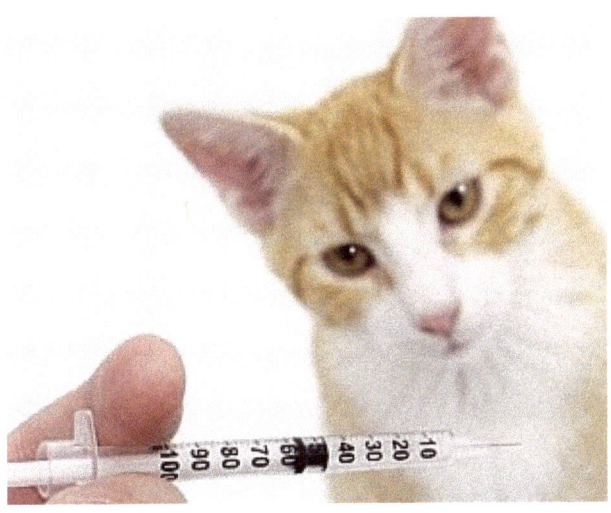

…..it is still the number one and best way to minimize or eliminate illness in our cats.

Vaccinating is not a method of treating illness or a cure for the diseases outlined in the pages to follow, but a means of *preventing* illness.

It has been proven that the risks of disease are far greater than the risks of vaccinating.

IMPORTANT REASONS WHY YOU SHOULD VACCINATE ME

When a cat is exposed to germs that cause disease, there is a delay in their creating the protective proteins (antibodies) needed to fight the infection.

While creating these antibodies, a cat can become very ill during this time and may be lost before they are able to fight the infection.

Also, infections may result in long-term negative effects.

In addition to preventing disease and loss of pets from disease, vaccinating lowers the cost of care of our pets. Diagnostic testing and treating pets that become ill is expensive and time-consuming, and it can be devastating for owners who love their pets.

Some feline (cat) vaccines available include:

F eline
V iral
R hinotracheitis
C alicivirus
P anleukopenia (distemper)
C hlamydia
R abies
B ordetella
L eukemia

There are other diseases cats may acquire; however, no vaccines are available for these following infectious diseases:

FIP- feline infectious peritonitis
FIV- feline immunodeficiency virus
TOXO- toxoplasmosis

The first vaccine discussed next is a combination vaccine including the first 3 vaccines parts listed above and is referred to as the **FVRCP** -known as the Feline Viral Rhinotracheitis, Calici, and Distemper vaccine. This vaccine is also known as:
- the kitty distemper vaccine
- the distemper combo with respiratory viruses vaccine
- sometimes the vaccine is combined with the next disease listed- 'Chlamydia' - and is referred to as the FVRCP-C vaccine

Rhinotracheitis

Feline Viral Rhinotracheitis (FVR) (rye -no- tray -kee- eye- tis) is a respiratory infection caused by herpes virus type-1. Don't be frightened, this particular herpes virus only causes infections in cats and will not harm humans. The virus can infect cats of all ages.

Rhinotracheitis is common where there are large numbers of cats- such as shelters and rescues and catteries.

Rhinotracheitis has a 2-5 day incubation time (the time it takes for the cat to become sick after being exposed to the virus) and is shed for 1-2 weeks when infection occurs.

Some cats can harbor and spread the virus all their lives even if they do not appear ill. These cats are called carriers.

Signs of rhinotracheitis include:

- coughing
- sneezing
- nasal discharge that can be clear, white, tan, yellow, or green
- irritation to the areas around the eyes- redness, swelling, discharge that is clear or white or yellow- this condition is known at conjunctivitis (con- junk- tiv- eye- tis)
- fever- sometimes over 105 degrees F
- secondary bacterial infections may make the signs and symptoms worse and cause the signs and symptoms to last longer than usual – or may cause permanent damage to the lining of the nose -resulting in unpleasant discharge from the nose for the cat's entire life

Additional signs include:

- corneal ulcers (the cornea is the clear structure that is the surface of the eye)
- keratitis (ker-ah- tie- tis) - an irritation and serious infection of the cornea
- dry eye- a condition in which insufficient tears are produced
- epiphora- (ee-piff- orr- ah) – excessive tearing- sometimes from irritation and sometimes from the duct connecting the lower eyelid to the nose (the nasal lacrimal duct) being plugged
- abortion may occur in female cats

The serious concern about this disease is that when kittens or cats are infected with this virus before being vaccinated, the infection can lead to lifelong signs and symptoms of upper respiratory infection- a 'cold' - and this will result in constant nasal discharge that is only temporarily cleared with antibiotic use.

This occurs because infection at an early age permanently damages nasal and sinus tissue. This causes the cilia – the small hairs in the nose and sinus- to be unable to clear mucus and bacteria. When this happens, the cat is then predisposed to lifelong bacterial infections. Many cats with 'runny noses' were not properly vaccinated prior to exposure and infection.

Vaccine is available to prevent rhinotracheitis. It is recommended all cats be vaccinated.

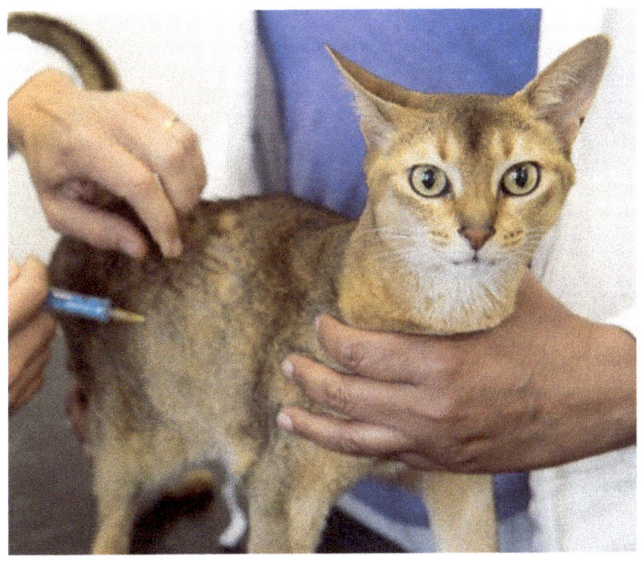

Vaccines may not eliminate all possibility of disease, however, vaccinating helps infection be much less severe and also decreases how long a cat may be ill from the disease. Also, the long term signs and symptoms of the 'runny nose' 'and constant 'cold' like symptoms are greatly reduced in vaccinated cats.

This author feels it is necessary to treat all infected cats to prevent secondary bacterial infections from making this disease worse and delaying healing in infected cats.

In severely affected cats, hospitalization and intravenous care may be required. If a cat or kitten is very sick and has a high fever, all of the above with antibiotics and oxygen may be required. Treatment for the other resulting conditions- such as disorders of the eyes- will also be necessary.

Calicivirus

Calicivirus (kah-lee-see virus) causes a respiratory disease in cats similar to Rhinotracheitis. It is caused by a virus of the family Caliciviridae.

Signs of calicivirus infection include:

- discharge from the nose that may be clear, white, tan, yellow, or green
- eye irritation- including discharge that may be white, tan, yellow, or green
- ulcers (open sores) anywhere in the mouth- the tongue, lips, nose, upper palate, and gums
- ulceration (open sores) in the intestines of the pet – which are not visible on ordinary exams
- loss of appetite- known as anorexia
- pneumonia
- difficulty breathing
- fever

While vaccination against the calicivirus is strongly advised, vaccinations may not stop an infection. However, this veterinarian's experience has been that the vaccine is helpful at protecting our cats. Infection can occur in cat of any age, but young kittens have been found to be most susceptible to calicivirus.

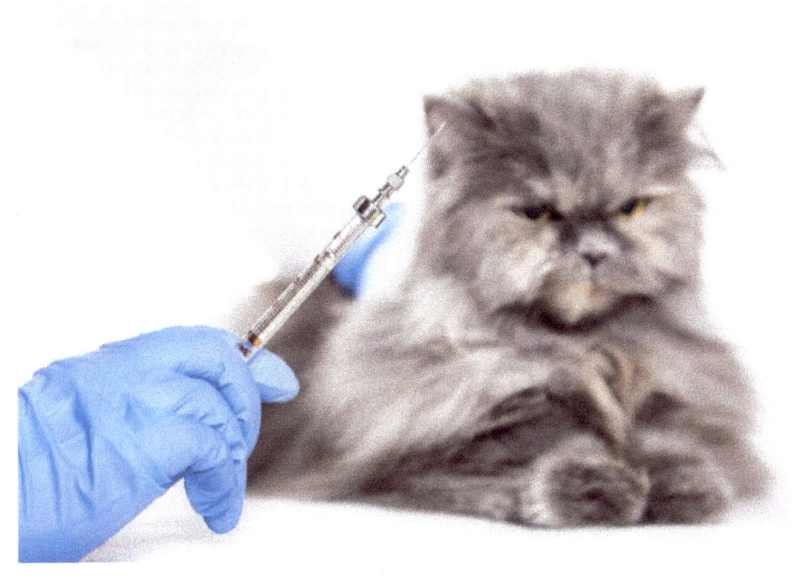

It is recommended to vaccinate and use caution when exposing cats to other cats.

Panleukopenia

Feline Panleukopenia Virus (Pan- luke- oh- peen- ee- knee- ah) (FPV) - also called feline – or kitty- distemper.

The feline distemper virus is very easily transmitted from one cat to another. It is life threatening to cats because it affects blood cells in the infected cat's body as well as the intestines, bone marrow and stem cells of a developing fetus. Red blood cells and white blood cells are discussed in chapter 11. These cells are necessary for the health of the cat or kitten and without sufficient amounts of them the kitten or cat will be lost.

An infection with panleukopenia results in a decrease in red blood cells- which carry oxygen to all areas of the body, white blood cells- which fight infection, and platelets – which clot blood.

Signs of Panleukopenia (distemper) include:

- vomiting
- diarrhea with blood
- dehydration – loss of body fluids
- weight loss
- high fever
- infection of any kind- respiratory, skin, and others
- anemia (low numbers of red blood cells)
- depression
- weakness – including the inability to walk
- rough hair coat
- decreased or no appetite
- hiding
- there is a high chance of cat/kitten loss with this virus

WARNING!

There is danger if pregnant cats are vaccinated with panleukopenia vaccine. If a pregnant cat is infected with the panleukopenia virus or is vaccinated with panleukopenia vaccine, the kittens may have impairment in the development of the area of the brain called the cerebellum (sara-bell-um). This is the back section of the brain and is responsible for muscle coordination.

Cerebellar hypoplasia (sara-bell-ar) (hipe-oh-play-sia) -is the condition resulting from panleukopenia infection or vaccination. Kittens affected early in the pregnancy are more affected than kittens affected later in the pregnancy.

Signs of cerebellar hypoplasia in kittens are that they are uncoordinated and unable to control their muscular activity. In mild cases, the kitten walks in a 'high stepping' manner and appears intoxicated or imbalanced. In severe cases, they cannot walk or eat or drink and may not survive.

Feline Leukemia

Feline leukemia (loo- kee-me-ah) virus- is a virus that causes cancer in cats.

Feline leukemia virus (FeLV) is a disease that impairs the cat's immune system (the system that protects them against infections) and causes certain types of cancer- such as lymphoma and leukemia. This virus infection was at one time responsible for a majority of deaths in household cats, affecting all breeds.

Cats at high risk of infection include:

- cats or kittens living with infected cats or with cats of unknown infection status
- cats or kittens that are allowed outdoors unsupervised, where they may be bitten by an infected cat
- kittens born to infected mothers

Response to infection with feline leukemia virus varies and includes:

    a. the infected cat or kitten may make their own protection against the virus and never show signs of illness or infection
    b. the infected cat or kitten may hide the virus- known as a latent infection- where the virus stays in the pet's body tissues- such as the bone marrow – but the cat or kitten is not sick
    c. the infected cat may become sick with the disease of leukemia or lymphoma

If a cat or kitten becomes ill, signs of the leukemia vary and include:

- loss of appetite – which leads to
- slow but progressive weight loss, followed by severe wasting of the muscles when the disease is advanced
- poor coat condition
- enlarged lymph nodes
- fever
- pale gums and other mucous membranes
- sores (ulcers) in the mouth (stomatitis) or gums (gingivitis)
- infection anywhere in the body- mostly of the upper respiratory tract- the nose and throat- however, can be in the urine or the skin as well
- diarrhea
- seizures, behavior changes, weakness, staggering, drooling
- in pregnant cats- abortion of the kittens or an inability to deliver the kittens may be seen

For many years leukemia was a common and devastating disease in cats, but now…

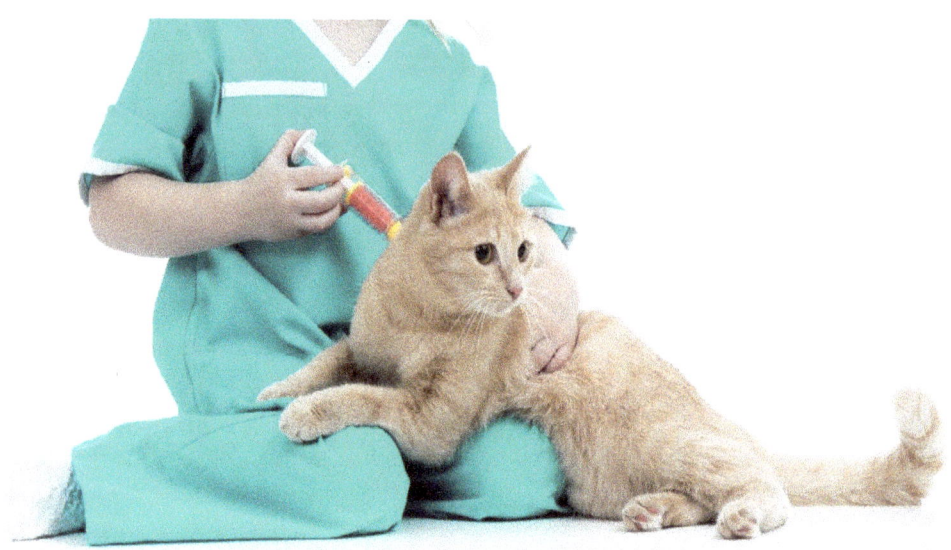

…Vaccine is available and has been effective in reducing the number of infected cats.

Chlamydia

Feline Chlamydia –(klah- mid- ee- ah) or Chylamydiosis (klah- mid- ee - oh- sis) refers to a bacteria based chronic respiratory infection, caused by the *Chlamydia psittaci* bacterium.

Do not be afraid, this is not related to the human Chlamydia bacteria.

Signs of Chlamydia include:
- watery eyes
- runny nose
- discharge from the eyes or nose that is white, yellow, green or tan
- sneezing
- coughing

In severe infections signs may include:
- lack of appetite
- loss of weight
- fever
- difficulty breathing
- possible pneumonia if not treated

Yes! ......

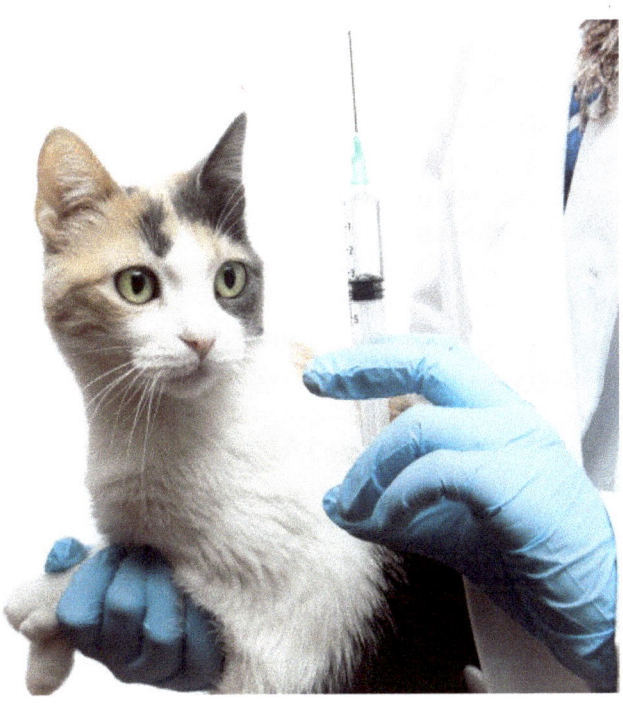

There is a vaccine available against Chlamydia infection in cats.

Feline Infectious Peritonitis

Feline infectious peritonitis (FIP) – (pear- it- tone- eye-tis) is a disease in cats caused by a corona virus.

This corona virus is devastating when cats are infected and if they become sick, it usually causes loss of the pet because it is incurable.

There are 2 forms of infectious peritonitis that may occur:

WET form- more common- signs include:
- fluid in the chest/abdomen
- difficulty breathing
- lack of appetite
- fever
- weight loss
- jaundice- yellow coloring to the skin, mouth and eyes

DRY form – signs include:
- lack of appetite
- fever
- jaundice – yellow coloring of the skin, mouth, and eyes
- diarrhea
- weight loss
- eye disease – blindness, blood in the eyes or cloudy eyes
- neurological - change in behavior, staggering, weakness

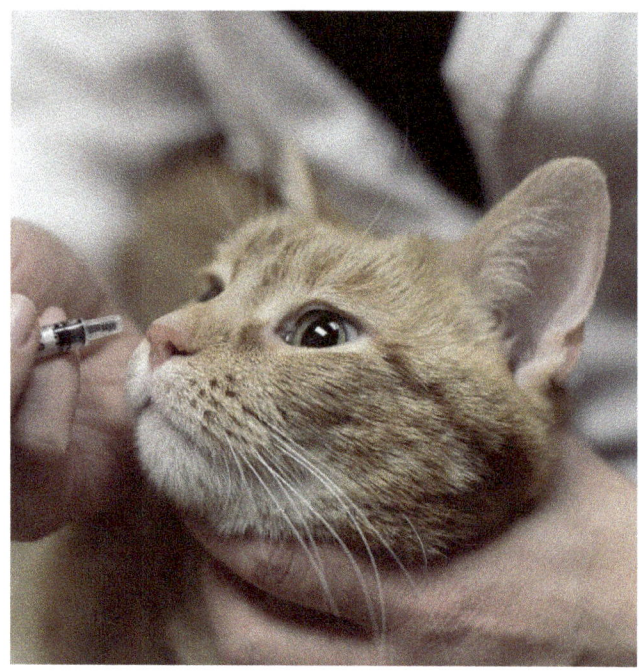

A nasally administered vaccine for FIP is available but controversial and may not be proven to be highly effective. There are experimental medications being manufactured that may be available at some point in time.

Feline Immunodeficiency Virus (FIV)

Feline immunodeficiency virus (FIV) (feline im-u-no-deficiency) is a viral infection in cats that - similar to HIV in humans- causes immunodeficiency disease.

Immunodeficiency means the pet's body is unable to develop a normal immune response when exposed to infections. As a result of immunodeficiency, most infected cats do not show symptoms and have normal life expectancy; however they are at risk for developing other infections – such as respiratory infections as well as infection in the blood, urine, or skin. Infected cats or kittens are also more at risk of developing any type of cancer- including lymphoma and leukemia.

Many cats infected show no signs of illness at all, however, Signs of FIV may include:

- infections of any type- respiratory infections as well as skin, eyes, ears, and urine infection.
- this disease may appear like feline leukemia virus (FeLV) infected cats or kittens
- growths (cancers) of any type and on any area of the pet's body
- mild to moderately enlarged lymph nodes
- irritation of the gums of the mouth and/or the teeth
- eye disease –of the surface of the cornea or deeper structures of the front part of the eye, including the iris (the colored part of the eye) and glaucoma (where eye pressure is elevated) is possible
- kidney insufficiency or failure
- diarrhea
- fever
- loss of weight and wasting away - especially in later stages
- nervous system abnormalities – such as not sleeping well, behavioral changes (such as pacing and aggression), decreased or loss of vision and hearing, or weakness, staggering, drooling

Rabies

Rabies is a serious and devastating disease of warm-blooded animals—including humans—that is caused by a virus called a rhabdo (rabb-doe) virus.

Rabies virus magnified

There is no cure for rabies in pets.

Rabies is transmitted between warm-blooded animals by bites or exposure to the saliva of an animal that has rabies. These warm-blooded animals include other dogs, cats, raccoons, skunks, foxes, bats, and even horses and cattle. Essentially any warm-blooded animal can contract rabies.

Rabies virus travels in nerve cells to the brain of an infected animal. This infection in the brain is responsible for the symptoms seen with rabies infection.

There are 2 forms of rabies-

1. **The paralytic form** – early rabies- mild weakness or other neurological signs such as loss of coordination followed by paralysis – the inability to walk.

2. **The furious form**- later form- where the pet may show signs of aggression or extreme behavioral changes- and may even attack.

Some signs of rabies in cats infected with the virus include:

- fever
- seizures
- inability to walk
- fear of water
- breathing with their mouth open and drooling
- inability to swallow
- weak and uncoordinated
- any change in behavior- either are now unusually quiet and shy or the opposite- unusually aggressive
- excitable
- a change in the cat's voice

Yes, the safest way to protect against rabies infection is….

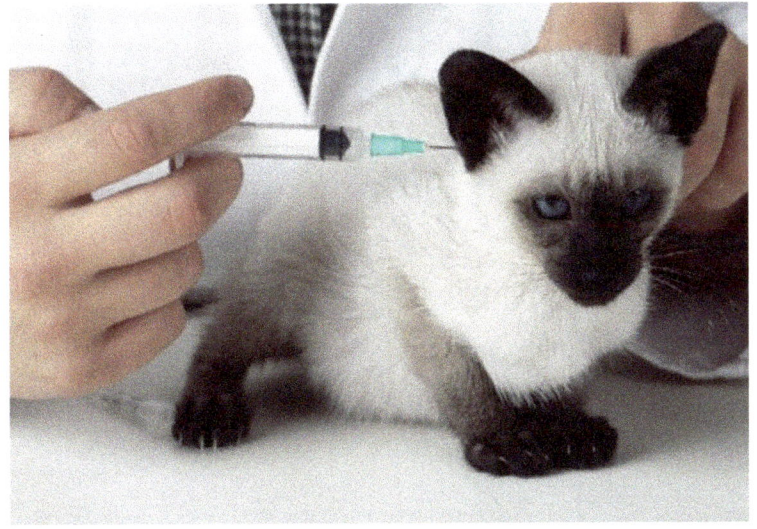

…vaccination.

Since there is no treatment for rabies, and humans can acquire rabies, health departments and governments around the country recommend and may require vaccinating all eligible animals for rabies. As noted, it is important to know that rabies is a disease that may affect humans.

Bordetella

Bordetella (board ah tell ah) - in cats is an infection caused by the bacteria *Bordetella bronchiseptica*.

Bordetellosis is easily spread in kennels and is most severe in young kittens (less than six weeks old) and in kittens living in unclean conditions. However, any cat with a pre-existing airway disease (e.g., feline herpes virus or calicivirus infections) is susceptible to Bordetellosis, no matter how old it is. Cats may have no signs of illness, however, can still spread the infection as carriers.

Signs of Bordetella infection in cats and kittens include:

- fever
- weakness
- sneezing
- discharge from the nose or eyes
- loss of appetite (anorexia)
- difficulty breathing – may even be trying to breath with an open mouth
- cough
- wheezing sound while breathing
- possible pneumonia

Yes! There is a nasal vaccine for cats ….

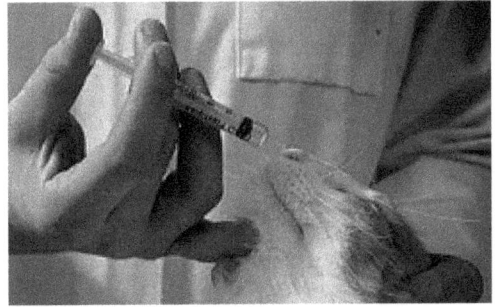

The effectiveness of the vaccine may be uncertain, however, it is recommended along with keeping cats and kittens from other pets with bordetella infection.

Toxoplasmosis

Toxoplasmosis (toxo- plaz-moe-sis) - is a disease caused by a protozoa parasite, *Toxoplasma gondii*.

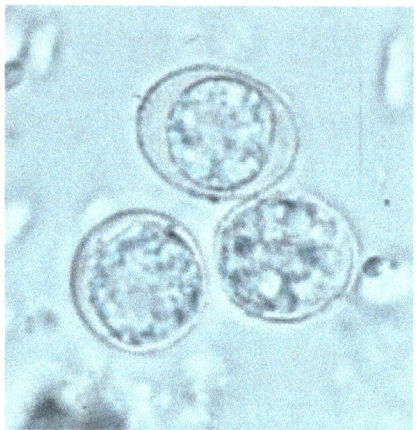

Toxoplasmosis is a disease that affects many animals and even humans; however, the parasite can only reproduce in cats. This means that in addition to being infected with toxoplasmosis, cats are the animal that sheds the 'oocysts' - the eggs that create new toxo organisms- in their feces (poop). These eggs are able to survive in the environment for months- which means many animals are at risk for ingesting them.

There are no signs or symptoms of illness in most cats infected with toxoplasmosis unless they are also infected with leukemia or immunodeficiency virus.

Symptoms that may be seen in a cat infected with toxoplasmosis include:

- fever
- decreased appetite
- resulting in weight loss
- fatigue (weakness)
- depression
- cold- like symptoms- runny nose, cough, runny eyes

Signs of more serious infection from toxoplasmosis include:
- difficulty breathing
- pneumonia
- staggering walk
- seizures
- tremors
- vomiting
- diarrhea
- pain in the abdomen
- jaundice- yellow coloring of the skin, eyes, gums, and more
- blindness due to toxoplasmosis causing eye disease
- neurological signs- such as personality changes, loss of balance, walking in circles, difficulty swallowing- resulting in drooling, sensitivity to touch, head pressing, ear twitching, loss of ability to control urinating or defecating

Preventing Toxoplasmosis

The best method of preventing toxoplasmosis is by removing urine and feces from the litter box daily and thoroughly washing your hands afterwards.

Additional Recommendations to prevent toxoplasmosis include:

- Do not give raw or under cooked meat to your cats or kittens.
- Do not give cats or kittens unpasteurized milk.
- Wash hands and food preparation surfaces with warm soapy water after handling raw meat.
- Wear gloves when gardening. Wash hands after gardening.
- Wash hands before eating (especially for children).
- Keep children's sandboxes covered.
- Do not give water from the environment to cats or kittens unless it is boiled.
- Do not allow cats to hunt or roam.
- Do not allow cats to use a garden or children's play area as their litter box.
- Remove feces from the litter box daily and clean the litter box with boiling or scalding water.
- Pregnant women, and persons with suppressed immune systems, should not clean the litter box.
- Control rodent populations and other potential intermediate hosts.

How is toxoplasmosis diagnosed in cats?

Laboratory tests are available to test for present and past infection in cats with Toxoplasmosis.

Can toxoplasmosis be treated?

Ask your veterinarian about treatment for Toxoplasmosis in cats. Most do not show any signs of being ill, however, and this may be challenging for pet owners.

No vaccine is as yet available to prevent toxoplasmosis in cats, humans, or other species.

Can I "catch" toxoplasmosis from my cat?

Because cats only shed the organism for a few days in their entire life, the chance of human exposure is relatively small. Owning a cat does not mean you will be infected with toxoplasma. It is unlikely that you would be exposed to the parasite by touching an infected cat, because cats usually do not carry the parasite on their fur. It is also unlikely that you can become infected through cat bites or scratches. In addition, cats kept indoors that do not hunt prey or are not fed raw meat are not likely to be infected with *T. gondii*.

In the United States, sources state people are much more likely to become infected through eating raw meat and unwashed fruits and vegetables than from handling cat feces.

For answers to specific questions regarding toxoplasmosis infection in people, please consult with your health care professional.

SPECIAL NEEDS FOR KITTEN VACCINATIONS

Kittens receive a 'series' of vaccinations because when they are born, they receive the protective proteins (antibodies) while drinking their mothers' milk.

These protective proteins are called 'maternal' (mother) 'antibodies.' These maternal antibodies protect young kittens from the diseases that affect cats, however, they do not last more than 14-16 weeks.

When mothers' antibodies are present, they interfere with a kitten making its own protection. Knowing this, veterinarians administer a 'series' of vaccines which are given every 2-4 weeks until the kitten is 14-16 weeks old- when mom's protection is gone and it is certain a kitten has made their own protective antibodies.

It is not as critical to consider WHEN a kitten's vaccines are begun as much as WHEN they are completed to insure adequate protection for one year. Check with your veterinarian for their recommendations.

Vaccine reactions

Yes, vaccines prevent disease or lessen the severity of disease. They lower the cost of care for pets.

Most of the time one cannot even tell a pet has received a vaccine, however …….

…..adverse reactions to vaccines can occur. These reactions are uncommon, however, can be alarming and even devastating.

Reactions range from mild soreness at the injection site to not playing or eating/drinking as well for 1-2 days after being vaccinated.

More severe reactions include:
- swelling to a pet's face
- diarrhea or vomiting
- fever
- hives- or any rash on the skin of the pet

Severity of signs may progress to anaphylaxis, which includes:
- difficulty breathing
- lower blood pressure – noted by a cat staggering or if they are unable to walk
- seizures
- shock
- coma
- loss of the pet

All adverse signs/symptoms noted by owners should be taken seriously and reported to their veterinarian, and if your veterinarian is not available, you should have your pet seen at an emergency clinic for pets.

In very rare instances a cat may develop a tumor related to the vaccine given. Any firm swellings in the pet's skin after a vaccine should be examined by your veterinarian.

Reactions can be frightening to owners and may discourage vaccinating. If a pet has experienced an adverse reaction to a vaccine, or an owner would like to prevent reactions in high risk pets, veterinarians may recommend pre-treating pets prior to vaccinating to reduce or eliminate the risk of an adverse reaction from occurring.

Chapter 4
Spaying and Neutering

SPAY - a surgical procedure to remove the ovaries and uterus of the female cat.

This procedure is also known as an Ovario Hysterectomy (OHE) or (OVH)

NEUTER - also called castration – a surgical procedure to remove the testicles of the male cat.

SPAY AND NEUTER ARE THE LOVING CHOICE

Good for your cat

Good for you

- no stress of heat (estrous) cycles
- no unwanted kittens
- no stress of cats running loose- possibly being injured or lost
- less cost for surgeries that are uncomplicated

Good for the community

- saves many dollars spent controlling unwanted animals

- decreases pressure on animal shelters to house or need to euthanize animals

- decreases the numbers of stray and homeless animals- a homeless life is a sad and dangerous life for pets- it is filled with hunger, diseases, exposure to weather, and being uncared for

- decreases the diseases in the stray population that threaten owned pets

REASONS TO SPAY

- no kittens
- no burden of finding good homes
- no strays
- less euthanasia of unwanted pets- cats can have as many as 3 litters of kittens a year
- no heat cycles for females and the unwanted behavior when in heat- such as loud crying, rolling over and over on the floors, trying to escape to the outside, urine spraying
- decreased incidence of mammary gland (breast) tumors – which are very serious in cats
- no chance of pyometra (a life threatening infection of the uterus)
- less cost- particularly less cost than surgery required for pyometra
- avoid complications of pregnancy and delivery of kittens in cats
- no males attracted around the home – or at least less
- decreased spread of disease such as immunodeficiency virus and others
- pets live longer

REASONS TO NEUTER

- no kittens
- less chance of unwanted male behavior- such as urine marking, fighting, howling, aggression towards other cats and possibly owners
- decreased injury- many intact male cats fight and abscesses result – therefore less cost at the veterinarians when neutered
- decreased chance of spread of diseases- particularly leukemia and immunodeficiency viruses as well as others
- decreased odor of strong urine
- less chance of leaving home and wandering- which may result in injuries such as being hit by cars, broken bones, becoming sick -some cats do not return home
- pets live longer

When to Spay and Neuter

When should you spay or neuter?

It is this author's understanding it is best to spay a female cat prior to any cycle or as soon as possible to decrease the potential complications included in this chapter for cats not spayed. Early neutering also prevents disorders listed in this chapter.

Most veterinary clinics recommend spaying/neutering between 5 ½ and 6 months. Some clinics charge higher costs for older, sick, or overweight pets because procedures on these pets can be more difficult, take more time, and may have more risk to the procedure.

Some animal shelters complete spays and neuters on all cats to decrease the unwanted pet population. Some spays and neuters are performed on very young pets before they are adopted.

Spaying and neutering prices vary depending on locations where these procedures are completed.

If prices quoted are more than expected, there are low cost centers that may be considered.

COMPLICATIONS OF SPAYING AND NEUTERING

Despite all the very good reasons to spay and neuter our pets, sometimes complications occur.

Uncommon complications may include:

- cost
- anesthetic risks
- infection
- pets removing their stitches needing more surgery- experiencing delays in healing
- inside stitches loosening requiring additional care
- small parts of ovaries not removed- resulting in symptoms of heat cycles
- and other complications

RECOMMENDATIONS TO MINIMIZE COMPLICATIONS OF SPAYING AND NEUTERING

Knowing there may be risks frightens some owners, however, as stated, there are many risks when a pet is not spayed or neutered that could be devastating to pets and owners. As with all situations, benefits outweigh risks.

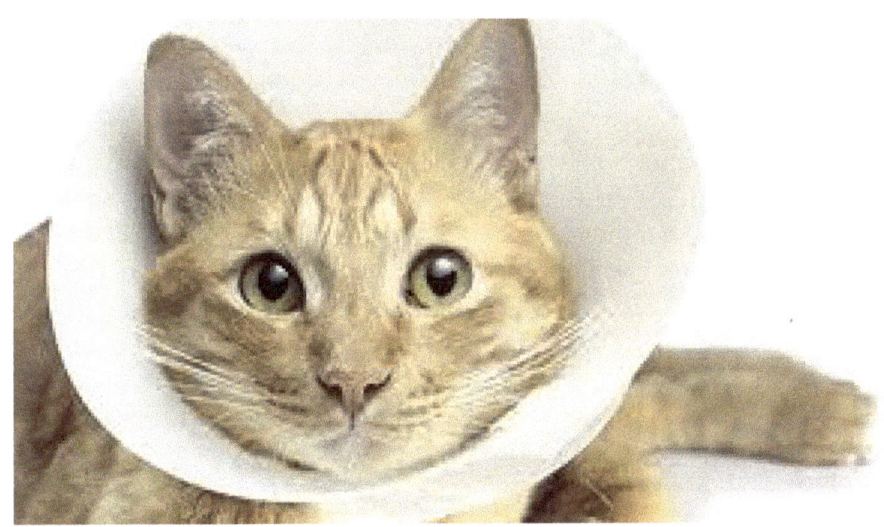

To minimize spay/neuter complications:

- have surgery completed on young cats
- provide a quiet place for the cat to recover
- do not allow the cat to run, jump, or other strenuous activity for the time recommended by your veterinarian
- no bathing the pet until the incision is healed

(More recommendations to minimize complications)

- check the incision – if redness, swelling or discharge that is yellow, tan, white or green appears, have the pet seen immediately by a veterinarian
- if there is any gaping (opening) of the incision have the pet seen immediately by a veterinarian
- do not allow your cat to become overweight before spaying or neutering
- schedule the surgery when someone can watch the pet for several days after surgery
- purchase an Elizabethan collar (AKA as an e-collar or lampshade) (shown on page 87) and place it on the pet to prevent them from chewing or licking the stitches placed – which can lead to opening of the incision and/or infection
- have your pet examined for any reason that concerns you

Chapter 5
Here's what to expect when your cat is expecting

For owners who want to have kittens or owners who did not read chapter 4!

FIRST THINGS FIRST ... GETTING PREGNANT

- estrous (heat) cycles begin in female cats 6-10 months of age, but can be as early as 4 months- heat cycles can last 3-16 days -cats come in and out of heat cycles on an average of every 14-21 days- each cat is slightly different
- visible signs of heat may include loud crying and rolling on the floor – as a general rule, no discharge is noted as in dogs
- some female cats may urinate more frequently or may spray urine on walls or furniture
- male cats may be attracted and found coming into the yard or around the house when a female cat is in heat
- the female may want to go outside to find a male cat
- male cats can make kittens at ages as young as 6 months
- most cats become pregnant without any help from their owners -if breeding purebred cats, you may need to consult with your veterinarian for advice
- pregnancy lasts 62-67 days- with an average length of 63 days
- it is best to make certain mom is over 1 year of age prior to breeding – however most pregnancies are not planned
- do not vaccinate pregnant cats with the FVRCP vaccine

YES! We're pregnant!

- nutritional needs of pregnant cats increase when pregnant and increase more as pregnancy continues and after the kittens are born
- pregnant and mommy cats need access to food and water at all times
- as the mother cat provides milk for the kittens, she gives them nutrition from her body -as the kittens grow, they require more nutrition from her -kittens take the most nutrition from their mother when they are 5 weeks of age and older- close to the time of weaning
- this is why mother cats need the most nutrition for themselves and the kittens by the time the kittens are 5 weeks of age
- mom will become very thin if she is not given enough food and water
- it is usually recommended to feed a high calorie food free choice such as kitten food during these periods of care- ask your veterinarian for their recommendations
- often nursing cats will lose hair during the time they are taking care of the kittens

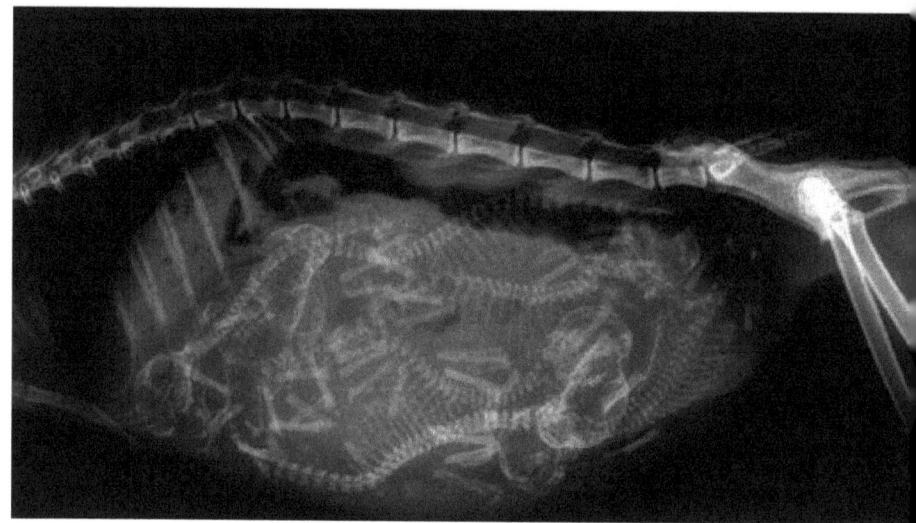

- The skeletons of unborn kittens can be seen on x-rays after 42-45 days of pregnancy (remember the pregnancy lasts 63 days)

- X-rays are beneficial because they

    - help make certain the kittens are healthy
    - help determine the number of kittens so everyone will know when all the kittens have been born
    - help determine if the mother cat is able to deliver all the kittens so help can be sought quickly
    - help determine the size and position of the kittens so if a Caesarean section is needed it can be done quickly

Ultrasound examination can determine pregnancy and number of kittens by the 14-15th day of pregnancy. Heart beats may be detected by 24 days.

The motto of kitten delivery is 'to leave no kitten behind!'

Being prepared

When it comes close to the time for the kittens to be born (whelping the kittens), it is important to be prepared.

Helpful supplies and hints are:

1. a whelping area- preferably a box large enough for the mother cat to be able to move around in with the kittens – mother cats seek safe places to have their kittens – help her get used to the box or basket you want her to have her kittens in- this can be done by giving her food or treats in the box/basket

2. a quiet place to have the kittens that is warm and free from drafts

3. make certain the kittens have a warm environment for at least the first 14 days of life because they are not able to control their own body temperature

4. a bulb syringe is useful if fluids in the kittens' mouths and noses need to be removed

5. clean dry towels

(Continued ways to be prepared)

6. a thermometer – her body temperature will decrease slightly just before she is going to have the kittens
7. reading material to learn about the kitten delivery process to know what to expect
8. be prepared to stay with a new mother while she is delivering and afterward as well
9. scissors to clip any long hair around the milk glands (the mammary glands) so the kittens can nurse easily
10. a calendar to help calculate the 63 days 'due' to deliver.
11. make certain everyone in the home understands that the mother cat wants to be in a quiet and calm place
12. emergency numbers handy along with the locations of local clinics and emergency clinic prior to having the kittens

ADDITIONALLY: when mother cats begin to become restless and make 'nests' for the kittens, they want to be secluded or they may worry and harm the kittens because they are frightened they cannot protect them.

THE THREE STAGES OF DELIVERY ARE:

STAGE ONE

The cat:

- may become restless and begin trying to find a quiet safe place to have the kittens – you may not notice this stage or this may happen up to three days before she has the kittens
- she may stop eating
- she may try to get to a very quiet and safe place
- she may begin to lick at her vulva
- she will begin to have a clear or cloudy mucous from her vulva – you may or may not see this if she cleans herself frequently

The owner:

- should set aside a private, quiet space with a whelping box for the mom
- have only 1 or 2 people around the mom and kittens during delivery
- stay with her and observe her - the way she is acting and the way she treats her kittens
- provide warmth as well as free access to food and water at all times even though she will lose interest in food just before she delivers her kittens

STAGE TWO

The cat:
- begins to deliver her kittens – the first one should be within 1 hour after labor begins
- kittens begin to appear at the opening of the vulva- some come out head first, some rump first- as long as they slide out, all is ok
- she may strain to push kittens out and she should remove the membranes around the kittens and lick them dry stimulating them to breath also
- mom should break the umbilical cord – if not, you can tie this off
- she should have a kitten at 10-30 minute intervals – sometimes it may be up to an hour in between kittens – as long as mom is comfortable, keep close watch
- she should begin nursing the kittens

The owner:
- stay with the mom
- have all the supplies close and ready to use
- keep the area clean and dry- membranes around the kittens cause the area to be wet and this can make the kittens colder
- be prepared

STAGE THREE

The cat:

- the mother cat should pass the placentas – usually one will pass with each kitten, but they may come after 2 or 3 kittens are delivered
- green and black discharge is normal AFTER a kitten has been delivered – it is never normal before kittens have been delivered
- the second and third stages may be ongoing and happen one stage followed by the other until all the kittens are delivered
- be prepared for a large amount of fluid to soil towels, blankets, and the whelping box during delivery-which need to be removed and replaced with dry ones after delivery
- the mother cat should clean all her kittens and continue to let them nurse

(STAGE THREE CONTINUTED)

The owner:

- observe the delivery of the placentas- there should be one for each kitten
- make sure the mother is caring for the kittens
- observe the mother for signs of confusion about the new kittens and help as needed- even if this means removing the kittens to protect them
- make sure mom does not accidentally hurt the kittens because she is confused
- make sure the umbilical cord is tied off with floss or clean thread if the mother has not done so- tie off 1/4-1/2 inch from the kittens belly when tying off the cord before cutting the cord from the placenta

(more stage three)

- if the sac is not removed by the mother cat, remove it from the kitten
- after the sac has been removed, clean and dry the face and nostrils of the kitten if the mother is not cleaning and drying the kitten (some owners use a bulb syringe to remove fluid from the nose and mouths of kittens)
- gently massage the kitten with a warm, dry towel until it is dry
- mother cats often eat the afterbirths – these may make her vomit – so try not to let her eat these
- make certain the kittens drink their mother's milk within 24-48 hours of delivery to receive the colostrum milk talked about in chapter 3 that has antibodies against the diseases of cats
- touch the kittens as much as possible to allow them to become used to their mother and be used to humans touching them
- keep them warm and make sure they are eating
- observe the mother's milk and mammary glands- the milk should always be present and white, and odorless and the mammary glands should be soft and light pink

When to worry

While most deliveries go off without a hitch, there are times an owner should be concerned and seek medical attention.

Seek help immediately if your mother cat begins to:

1. push without producing a kitten within 30 minutes
2. have blood coming from her vulva
3. have any abnormal or bad smelling discharge from her vulva
4. press her abdomen trying to deliver a kitten, but is unable to deliver one
5. not have all kittens delivered within 24 hours of starting labor
6. become exhausted
7. collapse
8. vomit
9. become unresponsive to you
10. have more kittens or more placentas delivered than one placenta for each kitten
11. have a kitten come, but not be able to deliver it from the birth canal completely and you are unable to gently remove the kitten within 10 minutes
12. stop delivering kittens for 2 hours when you know more kittens need to come

(When to worry continued)

13. have 2 kittens trying to be delivered at the same time
14. cry and/or appear in pain
15. appear depressed
16. have a pregnancy that lasts longer than 66 days
17. have a decrease in temperature below 98F or over 102.5F
18. concern you for any reason

What to do

In the event that the birth of the kittens needs medical care, a c-section (Caesarean section) may be necessary.

C- section is a surgical procedure in which an incision is made to open the abdomen; another incision is made to open the uterus so the kittens may be removed with the surgeon's hands.

A C- section should be performed by a veterinarian as soon as it is determined the mother cat is unable to deliver the kittens herself. Sometimes c- sections are scheduled for cats known to have delivery difficulty- such as the case in certain purebred cats.

A delay in seeking medical care may cause loss of the kittens and possibly the mother cat.

THE KITTENS ARE HERE!

After mom has the kittens, make sure:

1. the mother makes milk- the first milk will appear slightly yellowish and is called colostrum.- it is this early milk that has protection for the diseases discussed in earlier chapters

2. that in a few days, the milk will turn white and should never have an odor

3. to examine the mother's mammary glands (the milk glands) daily to make sure they are filled with milk and soft

4. to check if the mammary glands become firm, hot, red, swollen, bumpy, or have anything but white milk coming from them – if so, the mother cat needs medical care immediately

5. the kittens are always active, able to suckle strongly, and growing

6. the kittens are warm- cold kittens do not survive (air conditioning and kittens kept outside in cooler climates can be potential difficulties for young kittens)

7. any discharge that has an odor coming from the mother receives immediate care (this may be an indication of infection)

8. within 24 – 48 hours after delivery of the kittens you have everyone examined-some veterinarians give the mother cat an injection of oxytocin to help the uterus shrink down and rid itself of any fluid or left over afterbirths from the kittens and a sooner appointment may be necessary if the mother or kittens are showing any other signs than the normal signs listed here

CALCIUM CAUTION!

Mother cats' milk has calcium for the kittens. While nursing, a mother's calcium level may decrease in her body leading to a serious lowering of her calcium levels. This may happen at any time before, during or after pregnancy, however, most typically occurs 17 days - 8 weeks after delivery. The signs this may be occurring are:

1. shaking
2. seizures
3. muscle weakness
4. muscle tremors
5. inability to wake the mother up - coma

Any of these signs or any abnormal signs in a mother cat indicates a need for her to be seen immediately by a veterinarian.

Some recommend calcium supplements after the kittens are a few days old and to continue for weeks while she is making milk for the kittens.

How Old Do You Think This Kitten Is?

Newborns- have their eyes closed and their ears folded against their heads

-they are unable to walk or feed alone and cannot stand

-they weigh about 3-4 ounces usually

10 days old- they open their eyes between this and 14 days

3 weeks- their baby teeth come in and they are able to move around more but are still shaky, their ears are erect

4 weeks- they weigh an average of 1 pound and are beginning to play

12 weeks – they weigh an average of 3 pounds

BOTTLE FEEDING TIPS

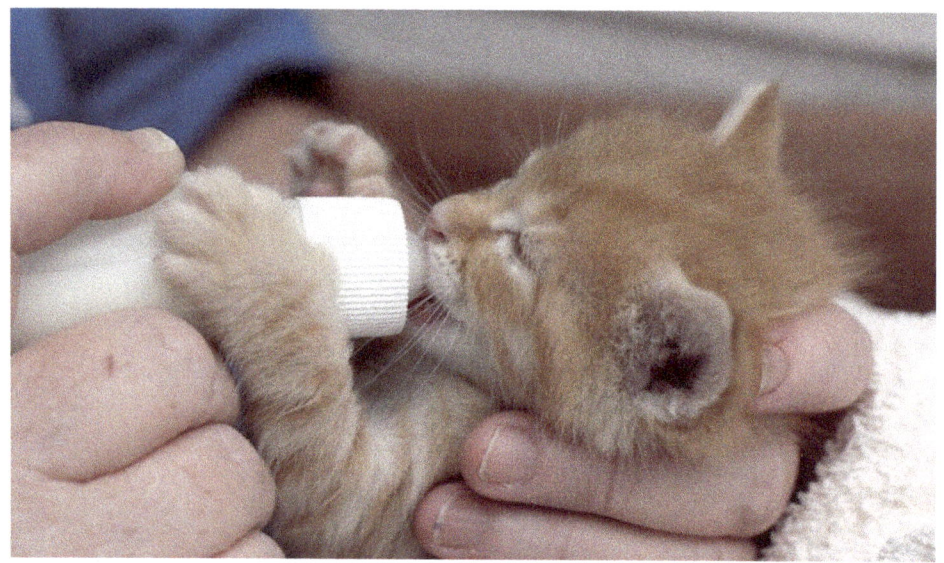

Orphan kittens may require bottle feeding.

If you are planning to orphan raise a kitten or litter of kittens, you should consult a veterinarian or a person who is very experienced in raising these young orphans. It is a great challenge and many areas of care need to be considered when mommy cats are not present to care for these little ones.

One common recommendation is to use KMR- kitten milk replacer- for feeding orphan kittens.

Some general tips include:

- give small, frequent meals
- make certain the hole in the bottle nipple is not too large- kittens may have milk go into their lungs and not their stomach if too large
- make certain the hole in the bottle nipple is not too small or the kitten with suckle and not obtain any nutrition
- you may want to consider a 1 milliliter syringe for easier feeding and switch to a bottle when the kitten is older- perhaps 2 weeks or so
- feed every few hours minimum until at least 4 weeks old- then you may decrease the frequency of feeding - ask an experienced person or veterinarian
- remember to boil the nursing bottles and syringes between every use- kittens that did not nurse did not receive the protection against diseases mentioned in chapter 3 and may be more susceptible to disease
- always wash your hands well
- do not give old or sour milk to a kitten
- there are homemade milk formulas if you are unable to purchase KMR – ask your veterinarian

WEANING

Although many kittens will eat as early as four weeks, some make take an additional two or three weeks before they express interest in solid food. Slowly substitute moistened kitten chow for baby foods or canned cat food. As soon as kitten chow is offered also keep a dish of water available for the kitten.

Medications While Pregnant

Medications may be necessary while a cat is pregnant and/or nursing her kittens.

Some medications may be harmful to growing or nursing kittens. And, even though not recommended during pregnancy or for nursing moms, some medications may be necessary to save a mother cat's life and may be used regardless of the effect on her kittens.

Some medications SAFE for use in pregnancy and nursing cats:

- activated charcoal
- artificial tears
- fenbendazole (Panacur)- dewormer
- ivermectin (Heartgard)- for the prevention of heartworm disease
- kaopectate for diarrhea
- lufenuron- (Program)- flea prevention medication
- hair ball medications (CatLax, Laxatone, LaxAire, etc)
- insulin (for diabetes)

Some medications NOT recommended for pregnant or nursing cats:

- acepromazine
- amitryptiline (Elavil) for behavioral concerns
- aluminum hydroxide—(Maalox)
- magnesium hydroxide- (Milk of Magnesia)
- aspirin
- buspirone hydrochloride- (Buspar) - for behavior issues
- butorphenol tartrate (Torbutrol) - for pain
- diazepam (Valium)
- cyproheptadine - for appetite stimulation
- diphenhydramine (Benadryl)
- enrofloxacin (Baytril) - antibiotic

More Medication NOT recommended for pregnant or nursing cats:

- epsiprantel (Cestex) - tapeworm medication
- furosemide (Lasix)
- prednisolone
- some flea products – such as Advantage
- methimazole (Tapazole) for hyperthyroidism
- metronidazole (Flagyl) -antibiotic
- phenobarbital
- orbifloxacin - (Orbax) antibiotic
- vitamin K
- amoxicillin/ trihydrate/clavulanate (Clavamox) antibiotic
- pyriproxifen (Bio-Spot) for fleas
- sulpha antibiotics - including Albon antibiotic
- tetracycline/doxycycline- antibiotics

Also NOT recommended for pregnant and nursing mothers are the poisonous plants, household products, and medications listed in chapter 9.

Always consult a veterinarian for recommendation of medication use in pregnant or nursing cats.

Chapter 6
Dental Care

DID YOU KNOW....?

- dental disease is the most common condition in cats
- all cats are at risk for dental disease
- many cats have dental disease by 3 years of age and this incidence increases with age
- the majority of owners do not provide essential dental care for their cats
- we want you to be of the small percentage of pet owners who provide dental care for their pets

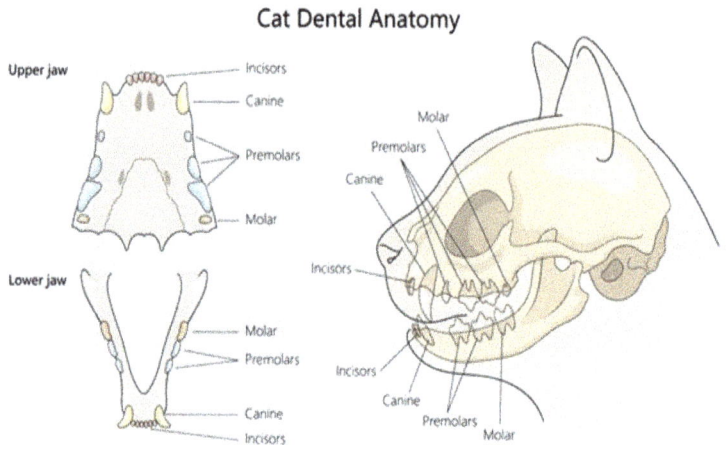

TOOTH ERUPTION

	DECIDUOUS	PERMANENT
Incisors	4-6 weeks	3-5 months
Canine	5-6 weeks	4-6 months
Premolars	6 weeks	4-5 months
Molars		5-7 months

Our pets need our help ...

Whether brushing or rubbing teeth, the key to dental health is to prevent the buildup of tartar on the teeth.

This chapter explores ways to save dental dollars and keep teeth healthier. Preventative care saves costly cleanings and possible extractions.

Aim- to keep pets in the 'no tartar' zone.

Cats present daily with the following stages of dental needs:

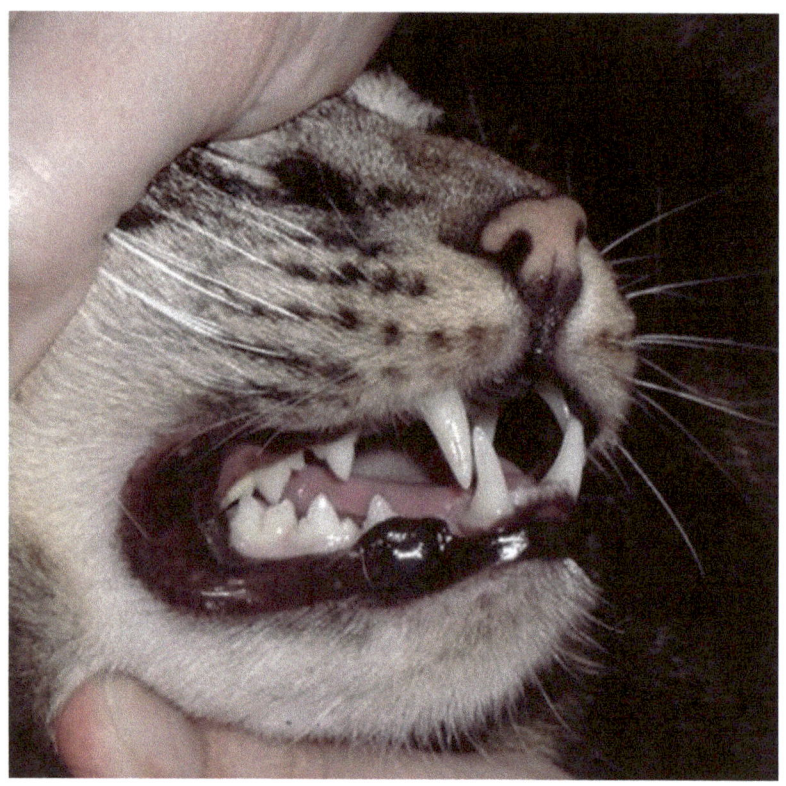

- no tartar

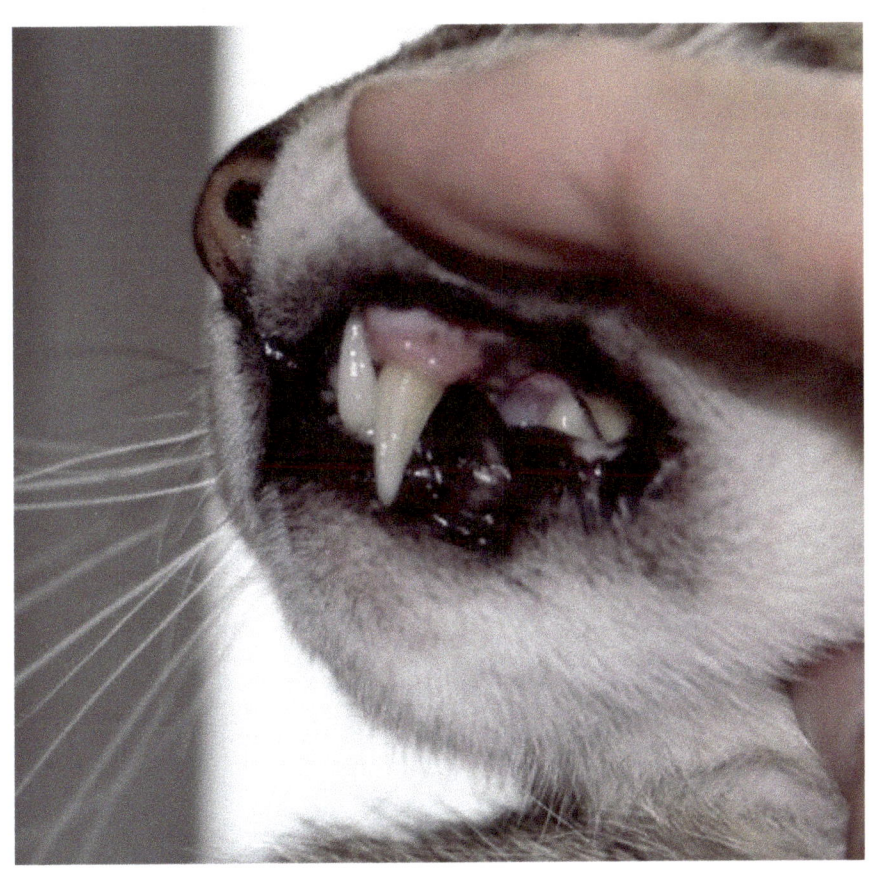

☐ mild tartar- this stage begins with plaque that accumulates and becomes rough and hardened with calcium to form tartar or calculus

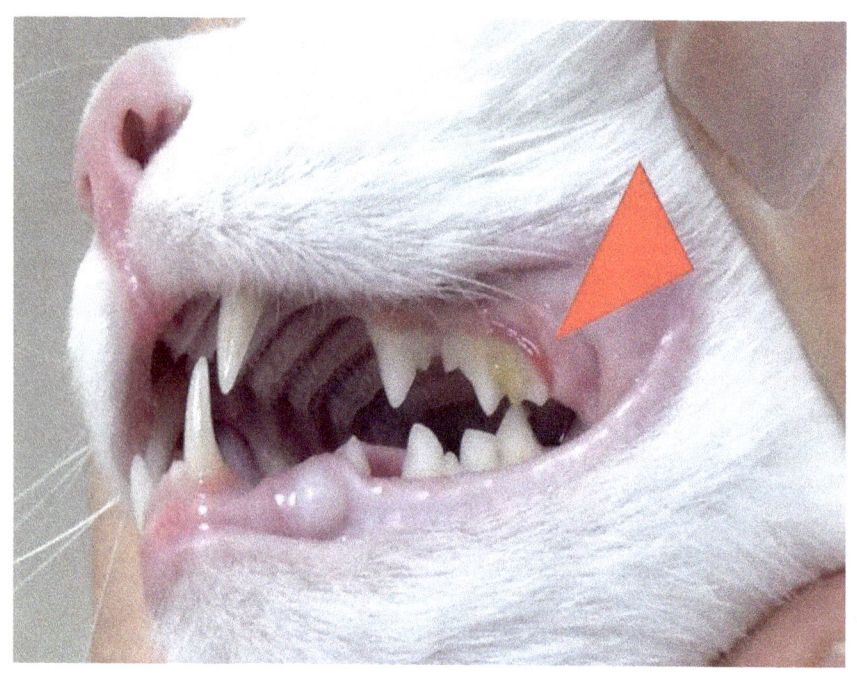

- more tartar- leading to gingivitis- which is an inflammation (irritation) of the gums that worsens over time

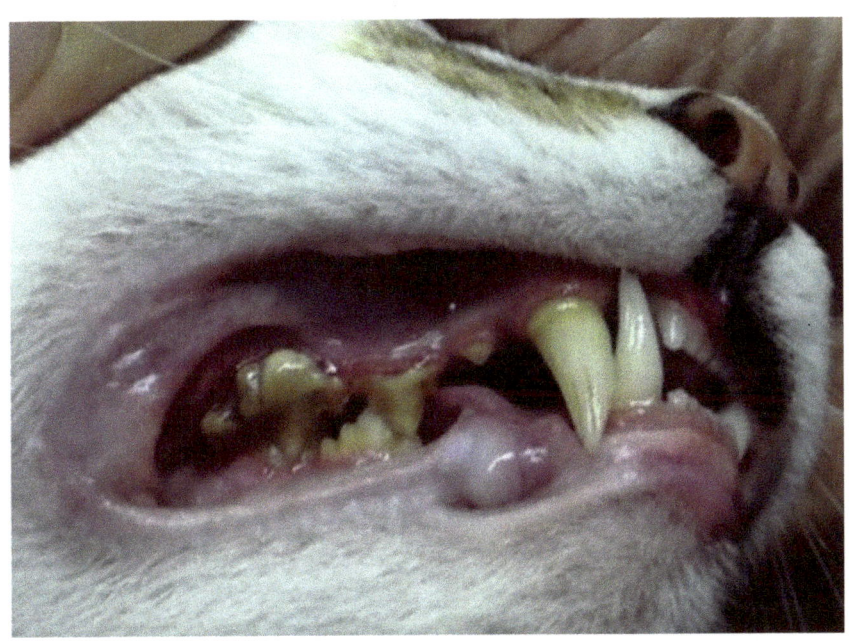

- much more tartar- as the accumulation of tartar progresses, the soft tissue and bone surrounding the afftected tooth are destroyed and the tooth then becomes loose- this is painful and leads to the loss of the tooth, however, this is preventable

Signs our cats need dental care

Despite the best care given out pets, tartar may still accumulate. If and when dental tartar accumulates, cleaning and polishing under anesthesia is necessary with the possibility of extractions

Signs a cat may need teeth cleaning are:
- bad breath
- change in eating habits- sometimes refusing to eat
- weight loss
- pain
- pawing at their face
- drooling
- loose and/or broken teeth
- exposed tooth roots
- red, swollen, bleeding, or painful gums
- sometimes facial swelling- especially under the pet's eyes
- obvious tartar

Teeth that are loose, decayed, and painful are removed. It is not recommended to allow these decayed teeth to remain in the mouths of the pets.

REASONS TO DO DENTAL CARE ARE:

- to avoid costly cleanings
- cat's with healthy teeth live longer
- prevent pain to the cat's mouth which may result in pet's not eating and weight loss
- reduce chances of gum and bone infection from germs in the mouth
- prevent bad breath
- as in humans, poor dental health can contribute to disorders of the cat's heart, kidneys, liver, or other body areas

TIPS FOR PREVENTING TARTAR BUILD UP

Several tips to prevent the buildup of tartar on pets' teeth are:

- dental chews daily help massage the gums and prevent tartar build up
- rinses – including antibacterial rinses added to drinking water
- toothpaste – use toothpaste designed for cats because human toothpaste is not recommended for cats
- brushing daily or at least 2-5 times weekly
- feed dry cat food (hard kibble) – this may be controversial for cat veterinarians – some recommend cats be fed wet food only – check with your veterinarian
- giving toys designed for dental health
- dental diets help some pets
- dental examination every 6 months
- professional cleaning when needed
- have decayed or loose teeth removed

GREENIES

Greenies aren't just for dogs!

BRUSHING

You can train your cat to allow you to brush their teeth.

Tips for brushing are:

- begin to train a cat when they are young
- talk soothingly to your cat so they view brushing as a reward and pleasant time
- use a small pet brush or wrap a piece of gauze around a finger – use circular motions on the teeth, always stroking in a downward motion

SOME INCLUDED DEFINITIONS

- **Periodontal disease** is a painful bacterial infection of the tissue around the tooth between the tooth and the gum that can result in tooth loss and spread infection to the rest of the body. Signs are loose teeth, bad breath, tooth pain, sneezing and nasal discharge. Periodontal disease has progressive stages that are reversible and preventable.
- **Gingivitis** is an inflammation of the gums caused mainly by accumulation of plaque, tartar and disease-producing bacteria above and below the gum line. Signs include bleeding, red, swollen gums and bad breath. It is reversible and preventable with regular teeth cleanings.
- **Halitosis**—or bad breath—can be the first sign of a mouth problem and is caused by bacteria growing from food particles caught between the teeth or by gum infection. Regular tooth-brushings are a great solution.
- **Swollen gums** develop when tartar builds up and food gets stuck between the teeth. Regularly brushing your cat's teeth at home and getting annual cleanings at the vet can prevent tartar and gingivitis.
- **Proliferating gum disease** occurs when the gum grows over the teeth and must be treated to avoid gum infection.
- **Mouth tumors** appear as lumps in the gums. Some are malignant (harmful tumors that spread to other areas and may cause the loss of pets) and must be surgically removed.

Chapter 7
NUTRITION

Proper nutrition can
- help cats live longer
- help prevent dental disease and overweight cats
- help prevent arthritis and the pain associated with arthritis

GOAL in providing nutrition: is to provide proper nutrition for cats for all stages of pet development.

OBJECTIVES OF PROPER NUTRITION FOR THE STAGES OF DEVELOPMENT ARE:

To provide nutrition for development of young growing kittens
- kitten diets are recommended for the first year of life

Provide energy for daily activities in young, active, and growing cats
- adult diets are available
- as well as active formulas have been created for the active cats

And provide for health and recovery as cats age:

- Senior diets
- Heart diets
- Kidney diets
- Food allergy diets
- Bladder stone diets
- Intestinal upset diets
- Low fat diets
- Diabetic diets

IN ADDITION TO THE DIETS INCLUDED:

Owners may also choose:

- grain free diets
- natural diets
- organic diets
- canned food only diets
- raw diets
- alternative protein diets- salmon, venison, and others
- and about 1,000 more

and last, but not least- weight management diets

Diets provide nutrition for all stages of a pet's life. Veterinarians help with these choices.
The focus of this chapter is different diets that help with weight management concerns.

Weight issues are often a sensitive subject for owners, however, weight is an important concern for our cats because:

        1. cats' weights determine overall health
        2. can predict their life expectancy
        3. and quality of life

It is proven that overweight cats are more prone to –

    1. heart disease
    2. diabetes
    3. bone disease including arthritis
    4. and many other disorders

Diet, along with exercise and healthy snacks promote great health and long life for cats!

The GOAL in weight management is - Not too thin, Not too fat, Just right

Weight management diets are available as:
- low calorie foods
- healthy weight formulas
- reducing diets
- satiety diets
- and others

BODY CONDITIONING SCORE (BCS)

BCS-is a scale used to evaluate body condition in cats- scoring is by using numbers from 1 to 5

The **BENEFITS** of lower calorie pet foods are …..

- less calories
- owners can feed a volume of food large enough for the cat to feel full
- pets do not have to beg for more food
- these diets provide proper balanced nutrition

When pets are fed less amounts of their current foods, the calories are reduced, however, so the nutrition reduced for the cat.

TREATS

- are a great reward for our cats
- are a great way for owners to bond with their cats
- help owners show a cat or kitten how much they are loved
- cats love them and
- owners love giving treats to their cats

Low calorie treats will not add additional and sometimes unwanted calories to a cat's diet.

Chapter 8
ARTHRITIS

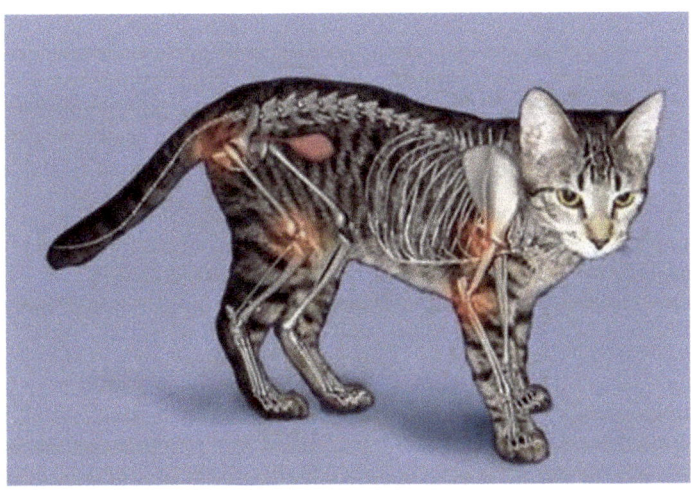

Arthritis is an irritation in a joint that is not curable and will continually worsen.

Arthritis is more common in dogs that cats, however, over 90% of cats over 12 years of age may have arthritis.

Arthritis causes changes in the bone and cartilage at the ends of bones that are included in joints (a joint where two bones come together).

Arthritis leads to pain - which decreases the quality of the cat's life.

Every age cat can have arthritis, however, mostly older and overweight pets develop arthritis. Cats that have been injured or had dislocations of joints can develop arthritis.

Hips are not the only joint in a cat's body that can develop arthritis- any joint may be affected – including the elbow, the knee (stifle), the spine, or any joint.

The different types of arthritis include:

1. degenerative (the most common- AKA - osteoarthritis)
2. rheumatoid (a condition where the body attacks its own tissue)
3. and infectious arthritis (caused by germs such as bacteria)

Predisposing factors include:

Arthritis can develop due to:

..injury, dislocation or infection in the joint. Extra weight also puts extra strain on a cat's joints.

- injury- including broken bones- by being hit by a car, being stepped on, and other injuries
- dislocating a joint- whether by being hurt or being born with bone disorders

However,

Most agree that cats that are overweight are more prone to arthritis and if arthritis is present, being overweight makes the condition more serious.

Arthritis caused by infection- bacterial arthritis- is a serious concern in cats because…

….cats – especially, but not limited to outdoor cats - occasionally engage in fights that may lead to bite wounds into a joint. This may lead to infection of that joint. If infected, the joint becomes swollen, painful, warm to the touch, and the cat will often not want to bear weight on the affected leg. The cat may have a fever and may not eat. The serious results of an infection is when the infection spreads from the joint to the bone (bone infection is termed 'osteomyelitis'). This will require intense veterinary care and the joint or limb may be lost. If the joint is treated successfully, arthritis will most likely develop.

Signs of arthritis include:

A cat that is arthritic may show many different symptoms. Essentially, arthritis causes pain. The symptoms that result from arthritis are a result of that pain.

Any change in your cat's behavior may be a result of pain. Each cat reacts to pain in a different manner.
Some examples are:

Reduced mobility:

- decrease in his/her activity and playfulness
- decrease in the frequency or refusal to jump up or down
- jumping up to lower surfaces than previously

- difficulty getting up and/or going up or down stairs
- stiffness in one or more legs, especially after sleeping or resting
- obvious lameness (limping)
- difficulty getting in and out of the litter box - therefore urinating or defecating outside of the box
- difficulty going through a kitty door
- difficulty walking
- swollen joints that may be warm to the touch
- decreased in the cats' muscle size due to not exercising properly
- carrying their hocks (the back leg joint) to the ground- one cause for this symptom is arthritis and this cause is often overlooked
- limited movement of some joints due to pain and muscles no longer stretching properly
- grating sounds to a joint- AKA- crepitus (krep- ih-tus)

Changes in activity:

- increased time spent resting or sleeping
- not hunting or exploring the outdoor environment as frequently as before
- some cats are less active and some more restless from the pain
- sleeping in different, easier to access sites
- reduced interaction and playing less with people or other animals
- difficulty finding a comfortable position to sleep in or a comfortable place to rest

Altered grooming:

- reduced frequency of time spent grooming resulting in a matted and scruffy coat
- sometimes over grooming of painful joints – leading to hair thinning or loss
- overgrown claws due to lack of activity and reduced sharpening of claws

Changes in Temperament:

- more irritable or grumpy when handled or stroked
- may be painful when picked up or touched/handled - certain positions may be uncomfortable
- more irritable or grumpy when in contact with other animals
- spending more time alone away from family/owners - while some are the opposite and spend more time around family members

Additional signs of arthritis include:

- decreased appetite - resulting in weight loss
- lameness (limping) - may or may not be noticed- some cats are very good at hiding their pain

The signs of arthritis in cats can be sudden, but most are gradual in onset. Knowing normal behaviors for your cat makes it easier to notice changes in those behaviors. This helps determine whether your cat is painful.

If in doubt about whether your cat is painful, seek veterinary care.

DIAGNOSING ARTHRITIS IN CATS

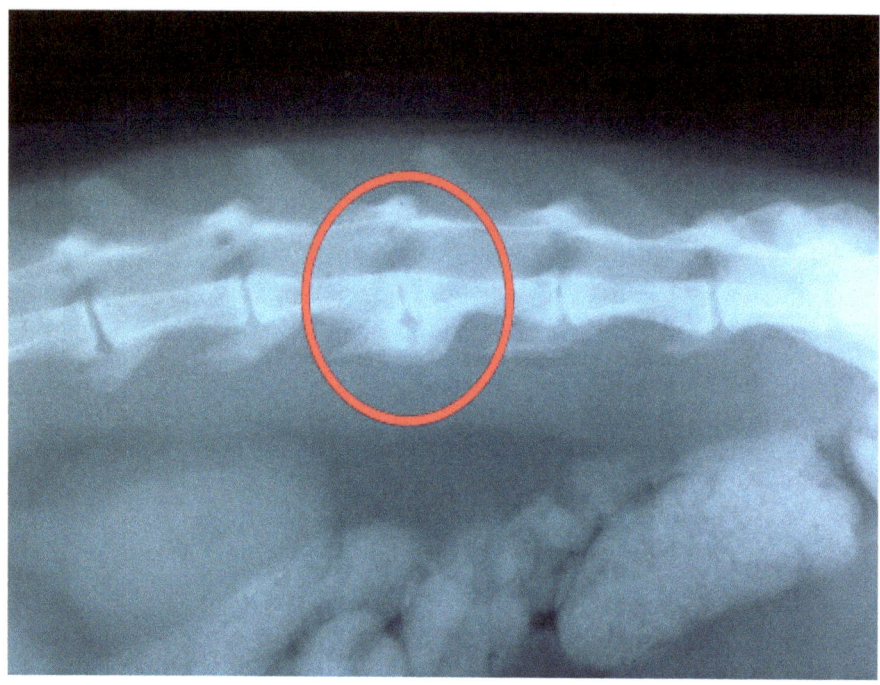

Radiographs are helpful in the diagnosis of arthritis in cats

GOALS for pet owners with arthritic cats are:

- having knowledge of arthritis
- being aware of available treatments
- knowing treatment recommendations change as pets age
- knowing the benefits and risks of all treatments
- knowing the proper administration of all treatments
- having a good relationship with your veterinarian

Treatments for arthritis include, but are not limited to:

Joint supplements may be effective in prevention arthritis and/or early stages of arthritis and include:

Joint supplements are available to all pet owners

When arthritis becomes more advanced, medications may be recommended.

Ask your veterinarian for their recommendations

Some common non- medication therapies include:

- heat application
- cold application
- manipulation of muscles and joints- as with physical therapy by moving the joints in all motions, exercising the legs and joints, and massaging all areas
- water therapy is also a great way to exercise a cat without stress to the joints- always have cat walk or swim in water with a life vest on and supervise the cat at all times

Other therapies and considerations for comfort include.....

- omega 3's added to the diet
- provide a cozy blanket or bed
- groom the areas that are hard for your cat to reach
- make sure it is easy for them to get in and out of the litter box as well as
- make sure they have easy access to food and water bowls
- keep their claws clipped
- provide ramps if able to avoid use of stairs or jumping on furniture

In advanced arthritis veterinarians may recommend:

- additional medications or
- surgery may be offered - such as hip removals, spinal surgeries or others

Research is always busy…

….. creating new treatments for arthritis.

Arthritis is common and can be costly. It may be preventable or delayed with early care.

Also, the most effective way an owner can prevent arthritis is managing their cat's weight.

Chapter 9
POISONS

Many common household foods, plants, and products are poisonous to cats.

Even therapeutic medication and flea products can be harmful if a pet is sensitive or allergic to the medication or product, or if they are administered incorrectly.

Sometimes owners give cats medication prescribed for dogs by mistake.

If a pet is poisoned, some signs include:

- vomiting
- diarrhea
- abnormalities in urine- in the color, odor, frequency, or amount of urine
- salivation
- staggering
- bleeding
- coma-unable to arouse a cat
- weakness
- seizures
- tremors
- change in mental status- appearing disoriented, confused
- difficulty breathing
- loss of pet

THE MOST COMMON POISONINGS IN CATS ARE:

- topical flea products used properly and improperly
- household cleaners and antifreeze
- poisonous plants

TOPICAL SPOT ON INSECTICIDES:

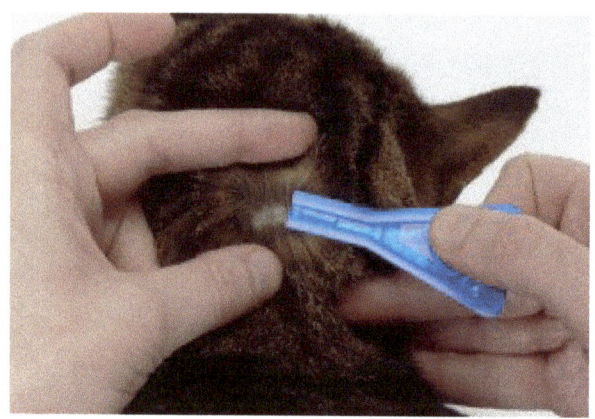

These spot- ons are the liquid flea products sold by veterinarians and in pet stores or on line pharmacies. Some cats are sensitive to the chemicals in the liquid and if a dog product is used on a cat, cats can become sick or lost due to poisoning.

It is important to remember that not only can the cat become poisoned if the liquid medication is applied directly to them since they are self groomers- it can be rubbed onto them after being applied to another pet and they can lick it and become poisoned.

Symptoms are serious and include excessive salivation as well as tremors that may result in seizures and loss of the pet.

HOUSEHOLD CLEANERS AND ANTIFREEZE:

Even if a cat is not directly in contact with these chemicals, if they walk on surfaces where the chemicals are and lick the chemical, they can become poisoned

Some examples of the poisons include:

- toilet bowl cleaners
- rust removers
- drain cleaners
- carpet cleaners
- detergents
- moth balls
- snail and slug pellets (metaldehyde) – even when placed outdoors under plants... and

The most lethal is antifreeze.

SOME HOUSEHOLD ITEMS TO AVOID INCLUDE:

- rat poison
- weed killers
- furniture polish
- matches
- liquid potpourri

HUMAN MEDICATION AND PET MEDICATION CAN BE A SOURCE OF POISONING TO A CAT

Some of these include:

1. fluoxetine (Prozac)
2. sertraline (Zoloft)
3. duloxatine (Cymbalta)
4. venlafaxine (Effexor)

These medications apparently have an attractive odor that appeals to cats.

Veterinary medications and other human medications that are poisonous to cats include:

1. carprophen (Rimadyl)
2. acetylsalicylic acid (Aspirin) in high doses
3. acetaminophen (Tylenol)
4. ibuprophen (Motrin/Advil)

SOME PLANTS AND SHRUBS TO AVOID INCLUDE:

- poinsettias
- ALL species of lilies
- tulips
- azaleas
- rhododendrons
- oleander
- ALL species of ivy
- amaryllis (Hippeastrum species and hybrids)
- chrysanthemum
- crown of thorns (euphorbia milii)
- cyclamen (kalanchoe)
- philodendron
- aloe vera
- geranium (pelargonium species)
- hyacinth (hyacinthus species and hybrids)
- primrose (primula vulgaris)
- baby's breath (gypsophila paniculata)
- holly (Ilex species)
- iris species
- mistletoe (many genera)
- naked lady (amaryllis belladonna)
- peony (paeonia species)
- and more

Many emergency clinics are available for assistance if your pet requires care. Always seek help immediately. The quicker treatment is sought, the better chance a pet can survive a poisonous exposure.

Always have emergency phone numbers available – Veterinary Emergency Clinics and Poison Hotlines

One Pet Poison Helpline is 800-213-6680

Chapter 10
TRAINING

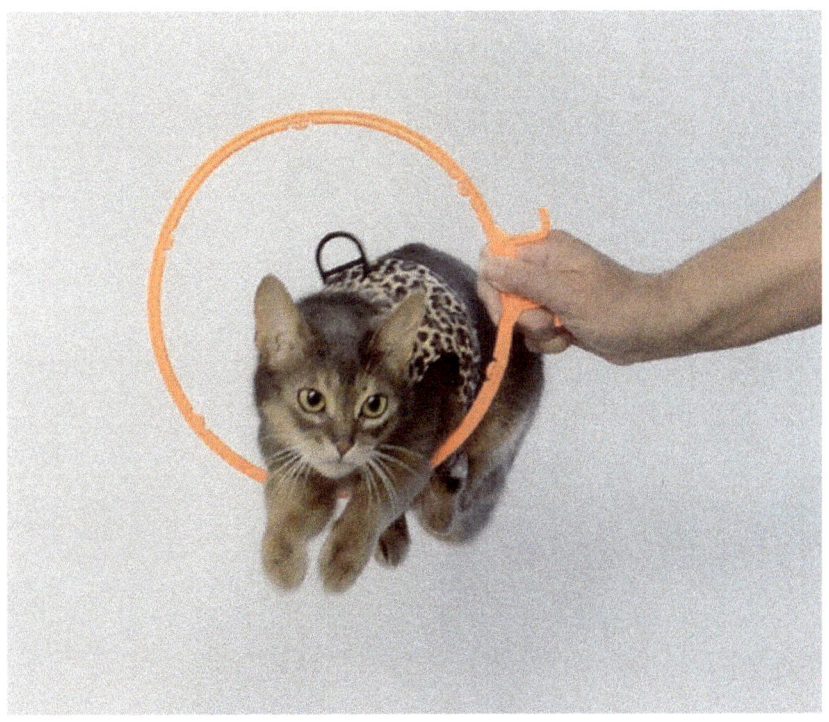

Who doesn't love a well trained cat? Actually, I guess the question should be 'Who has or trains a well trained cat?'

Some talented owners are able to train their cats to…

….do all the things a dog can do.

Like….. come, sit, stand …..

….wave, sit pretty, roll over, high five, fetch, and give kisses,

…some extra talented owners teach their cats to:

…..jump objects, run obstacle courses, walk on a leash……

Others teach cats to....

play chess or.......

….even...

…..play the piano, but....

As much fun as training can be ....

Difficulties with pet behavior may lead an owner to surrender a pet to a shelter.

It is sad when objectionable behavior that can be avoided leads to separation of pet and owner.

Cats are not born bad.

BEHAVIOR ISSUES FREQUENTLY ENCOUNTERED INCLUDE:

- aggression towards other pets and humans
- inappropriate urination
- jumping up on counters or furniture
- escaping out windows or doors
- eating objects that may become lodged in the intestines or stomach and require surgery to remove

SOME WAYS TO DEAL WITH BEHAVIOR ISSUES INCLUDE:

- be informed - get books from the library or contact a trainer
- be consistent
- be kind
- try to avoid the cat doing unwanted behaviors
- seek assistance early when a problem is identified
- if you are having a litter box issue-
    - make sure you see a veterinarian to make certain no urinary disorder is present
    - have 1 litter box per cat
    - keep the litter boxes very clean

- if you are having a scratching problem
    - keep the cat's/kitten's nails trimmed
    - have scratching posts in the home
    - have plenty of appropriate toys for the cat or kitten
    - consider covering the nails with soft paws

..if you have aggression concerns-

- ask a veterinarian for an exam to eliminate causes for the behavior- such as pain
- have all cats in the home spayed and neutered
- make certain there are enough food bowls, litter boxes, and toys
- don't hit the cat or kitten- but do try to separate fighting cats if possible

And if you are unable to remedy aggression or any behavior issue...

... you may need the help of a behavior specialist or medications.

SOCIALIZING CATS IS IMPORTANT

TIPS INCLUDE:
- start socializing a kitten when it is young- this is easier than when they are older
- slowly get them used to being brushed- with a hand, a glove, a brush, or a wand
- play with them often
- introduce them to many people and other pets that are safe as much as possible- especially before they are 6 months old
- brush their teeth or clip their nails from a young age to allow them to get used to this and not object when older
- pick them up as often as able
- spend time with them- playing and stroking
- allow them the time they need to adjust and learn
- know that some cats never socialize with other people or pets and they may need to be the only pet in the home

Our goal is to help keep owners and cats together.

Chapter 11
DIAGNOSTIC TESTING
A CLOSER LOOK

The first tool a veterinarian has to decide what disorders a cat may be experiencing is the physical exam.

The exam is important, however, does not provide all the necessary information to make decisions about disorders and care recommendations and a closer look is usually necessary.

Tests are available which help veterinarians make accurate decisions about disorders cats' experience- and therefore more accurate treatment recommendations.

Understanding the testing often recommended may be helpful to owners in making decisions regarding their cats' care.

Some common tests recommended are:

1. fecal samples (AKA poop samples)
2. blood tests to count cells
3. blood tests for screening body organs
4. measuring electrolytes
5. blood tests for irritation of the pancreas
6. thyroid testing
7. testing for kidney disorders – the BUN and creatinine
8. diabetes mellitus testing
9. heartworm in cats
10. hepatic lipidosis – fatty liver in cats
11. leukemia and immunodeficiency and heartworm testing
12. radiographs- x-rays
13. advanced testing- ultrasounds, MRIs, CT scans
14. skin testing
15. cultures
16. urine testing
17. ear testing
18. eye testing
19. and more

FECAL TESTING

Veterinarians examine feces (AKA-stool, poop, and other home spun terms) to test for several common infections such as:

1. intestinal parasites -'AKA 'worms' ... and
2. coccicia

Intestinal parasites common to cats include-

COMMON INTESTINAL WORMS AND THEIR SCIENTIFIC NAMES

COMMON NAME	SCIENTIFIC NAME
rounds	(Toxocara spp.)
hooks	(Ancylostoma spp)
tapeworms (tapes)	(Dipylidium and Tenia)

Various medications are used to treat each type of 'worm' a cat may be infected with.

Intestinal parasites require treatment because they cause:

- poor growth
- dull hair coats
- thinness in cats
- lack of energy
- diarrhea
- vomiting
- loss of appetite
- anemia (decrease in the amount of red blood cells in the body
- large- or pot bellied- appearance
- and loss of pets when large numbers of worms are present

An additional and important reason to identify and treat worms is because they can be a health hazard to children and adults.

ROUND WORMS "ROUNDS"

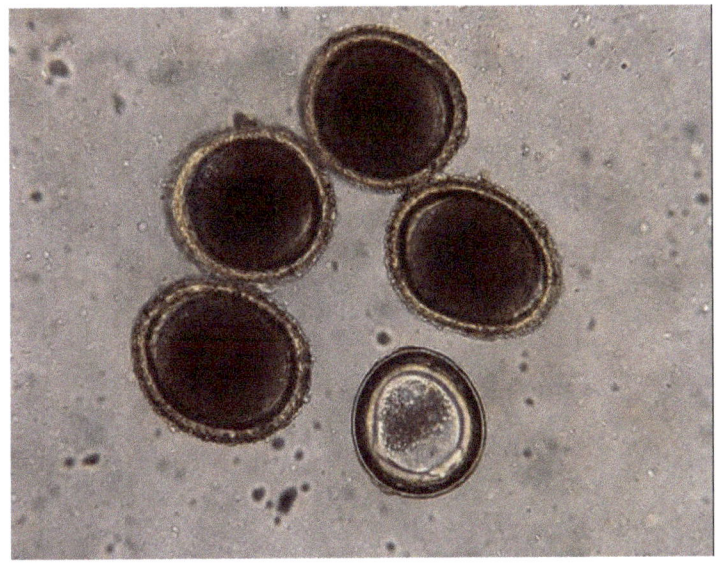

'Rounds' are the most commonly seen parasite in cats- especially kittens – they are transmitted to kittens from their moms through the placenta before birth and the mother's milk after birth.

Rounds can be seen as white curly worms in stool or vomit that look like spaghetti.

HOOK WORMS "HOOKS"

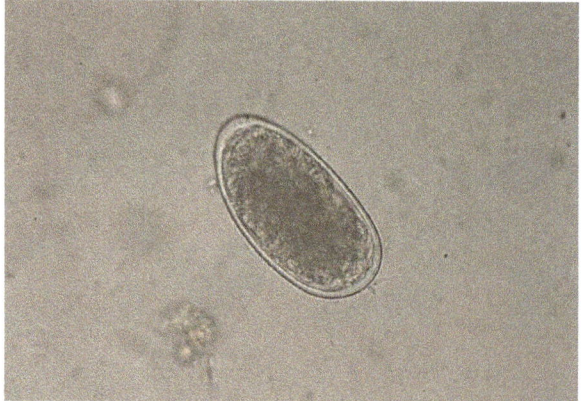

Hookworms are so small they can only be seen under a microscope.

They are serious because they damage the lining of the intestines when they attach there.

The main source of infection for cats is usually soil contaminated with stool of infected pets; however, some hookworm infections are transmitted in a mother's milk to nursing kittens.

Additional symptoms seen in hookworm infection include:

1. severe illness
2. anemia
3. blood in the pet's stool
4. poor absorption of nutrition because of the damage to the lining of the intestinal tract- which can cause weight loss
5. this worm can be life threatening if untreated

TAPEWORMS "TAPES"

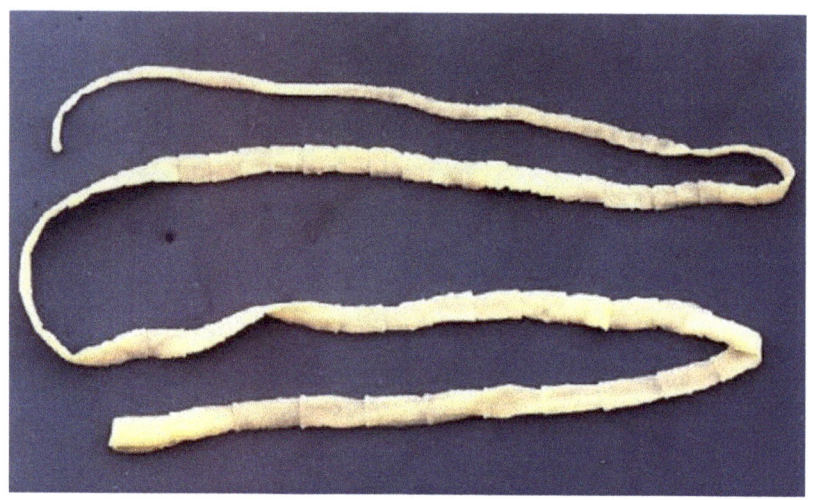

The 3 parts of a tapeworm are:

1. the head-which attaches to the intestinal lining
2. the neck
3. and the segments- which are passed and seen in the stool

Unlike other 'worms,' tapeworms are not passed directly from cat to cat- an 'intermediate' or 'in between' host is required for infection.

The segments are passed in the pet's stool, are identified as flat white worms or 'rice' on a pet's stool or hair. These segments contain tapeworm eggs.

These eggs are distributed in the environment and picked up by fleas and other possible 'host's (such as rodents).

When a cat grooms itself and swallows fleas, the tapeworms develop into an adult worm and attach to the lining of the intestines- creating a new infection and cycle.

Treatment is available for tapes and necessary because as long as the head of the tapeworm is attached to the lining of the intestinal tract, the cat is unable to digest and eliminate the worms themselves.

Tapeworms are not always detected on fecal examination, so many veterinarians treat when owners see these worms on their cat's stool.

Treatment is necessary because tapeworms can cause a cat to be ill or unthrifty.

Treatment for tapeworms is aimed at controlling flea infestations as well as treating the tapeworms

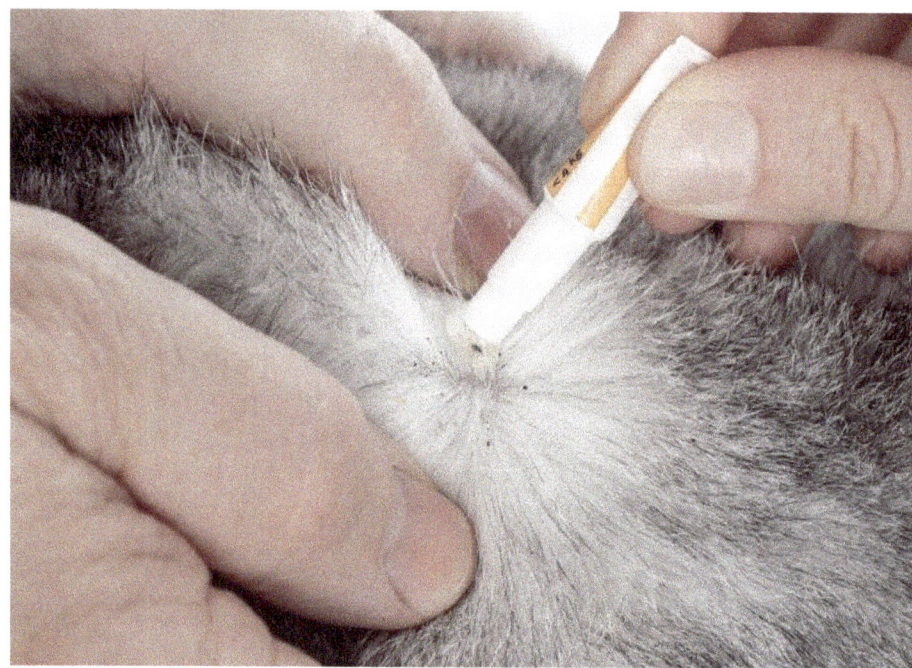

Recommended treatment for fleas includes:

- treating all pets in the home all year
- cleaning all surfaces and bedding related to the pet in the home
- treating the environment if possible (the yard)

COCCIDIA

When testing feces, another common intestinal parasite may be a concern:

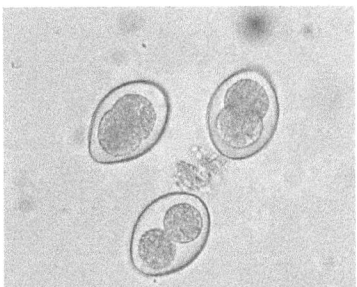

- **coccidia** is a single cell organism- (a protozoa) that can only be seen under a microscope

Medication is available to treat coccidia. Treatment is essential to avoid serious complications that can result with this infection.

BLOODWORK

In addition to heartworm testing, veterinarians may recommend examining blood for the following:

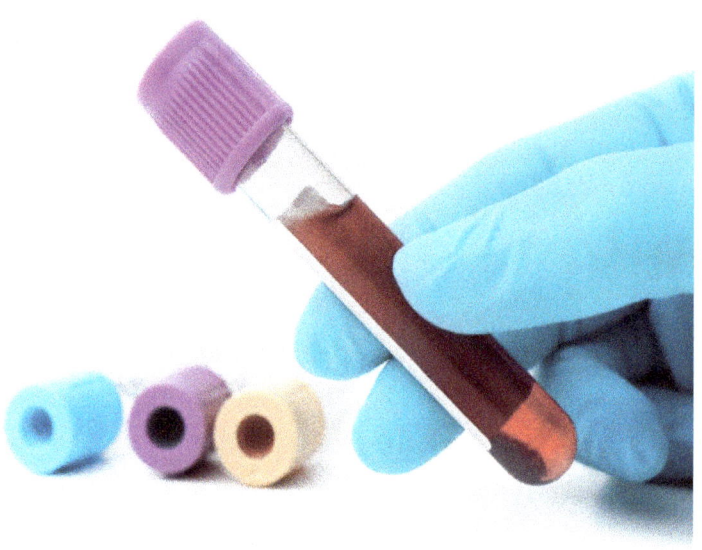

- complete Blood Counts- known as a CBC
- chemistry panels- known as SMAC, internal organ function, chem- 7,12, 15
- electrolytes- including sodium, chloride, and potassium
- pancreatic testing
- thyroid examination – most often a 'T4'
- diabetic mellitus testing
- leukemia/fiv/heartworm testing
- and others

Normal and Abnormal Values

Normal and abnormal test results have value to veterinarians in the care of cats.

When evaluating blood values, there are standards called 'normal' values. Health is when the values are 'normal' and disease may be identified when values are either too high or too low.

In addition, oftentimes, testing may be:

- conclusive - give enough information to conclude what is wrong with the cat
- suggestive - a disorder may be apparent, but need further testing to be absolutely certain
- inconclusive - some tests could indicate more than one disorder, so additional testing is necessary to be certain

Suggestive and inconclusive testing indicates a need for additional testing or referral to specialists for assistance with identifying disorders in cats.

FACTS ABOUT BLOOD

When blood is placed in a spinner and spun, it separates into 3 parts:

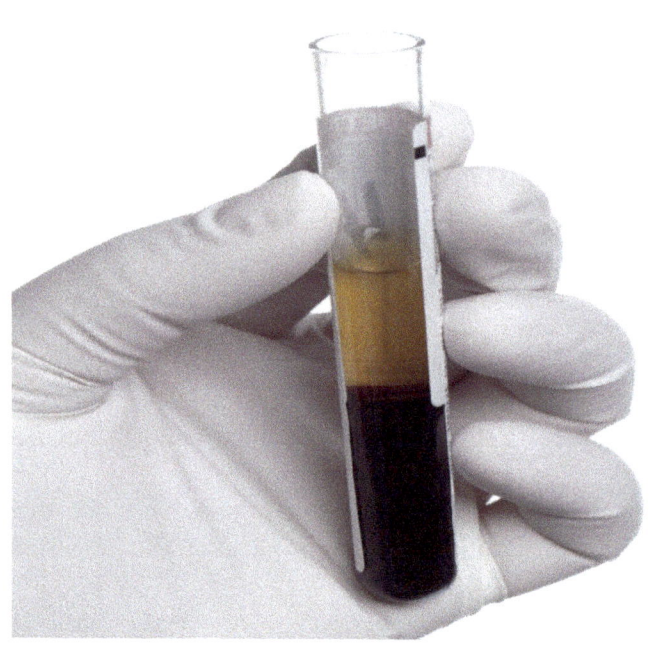

1. the liquid part that normally looks clear or slightly straw colored
2. the red blood cells – which settle to the bottom
3. the white blood cells - a small layer of cells which are usually in the layer between the liquid part and the red blood cell

These parts of the blood are tested

CBC- the complete blood count

The cells counted are:

1. the red cells- which carry oxygen n the blood
2. the platelets- which help with blood clotting
3. the white blood cells- there are several different types which help protect cats by fighting infection and other things (such as cancer)

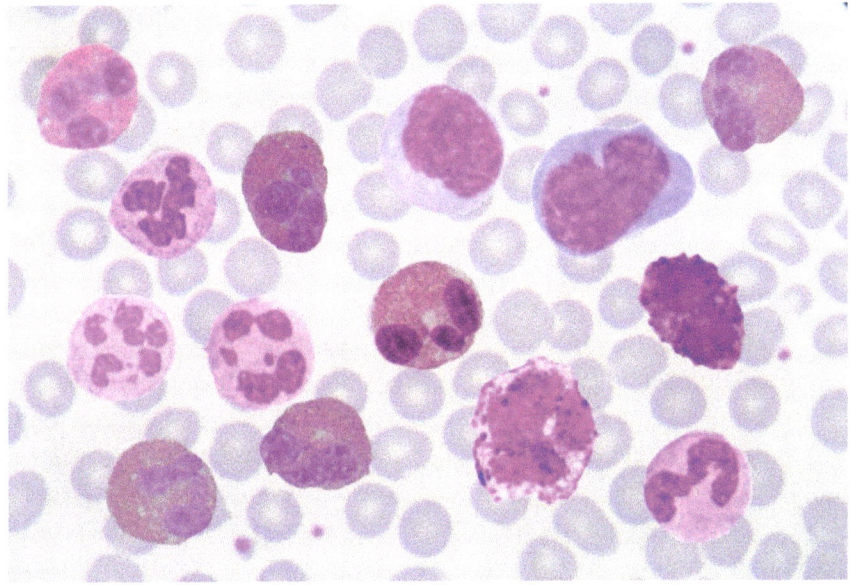

Veterinarians gain information when cell counts are:

- too high
- too low
- or just right (normal)

With this information, the veterinarian can create treatment plans for the care of cats.

CHEMISTRY

"Chemistry" tests are performed on the liquid part of blood and screen different items.

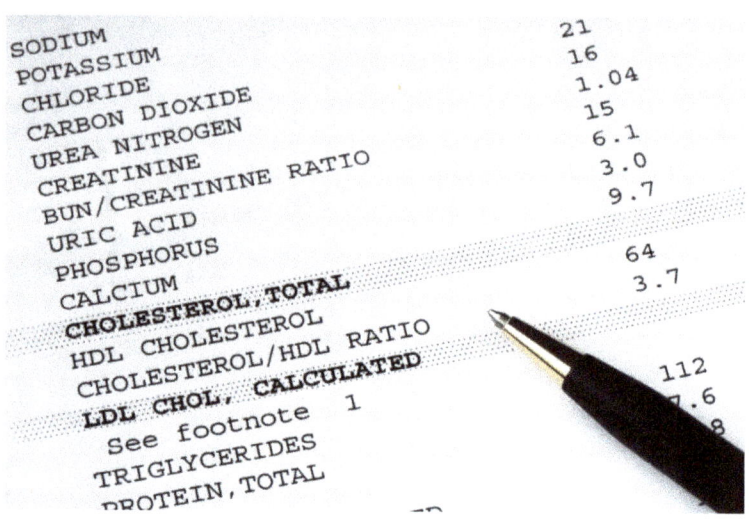

Some items relate to blood levels reflecting organ health such as liver and kidney health, and some values relate to sugar in the blood, calcium, and even cholesterol. When these screening values are not within a 'normal' range, illness is usually indicated as well as the need for treatment and/or further testing or referral to specialists to decide what disorders may be present.

Several different chemistry 'panels' are available – the number associated with the chemistry panel usually indicates how many items are being tested – for example-

Chem 6- tests 6 basic items in the blood
Chem 12- tests 12 items
Chem 25- tests 25 items-

And so on.....
It is easy to see that the more items tested for, the more information is obtained

Specific Tests for Chemistry Evaluation

As with the CBC- there are 'normal' standards established for the chemistry items tested for. Values that are 'too high' or 'too low' may indicate a need for treatment

Some 'chemistry' items tested are:

- Glucose-AKA – the blood sugar
- Creatinine- screens for kidney health
- BUN- the 'blood urea nitrogen' -screens for kidney health
- ALT-(alanine aminotransferase)- screens for liver health
- AST- (aspartate animotransferase) -screens for liver health
- GGT- (gamma glutamyltransferase) screens for liver health
- Albumin- is a protein found in the blood
- Gobulin- is a protein found in the blood
- Alkaline Phosphatase-screens for liver and/or muscle and bone health
- Cholesterol- measures the amount of cholesterol in the pet's body
- Total bilirubin- screens for liver and gall bladder and red blood cell health
- Phosphorus- measures the level of phosphorous in the pet's blood
- Amylase – screens for pancreatic health
- Lipase- screens for pancreatic health

ELECTROLYTES

Electrolytes are dissolved chemicals with electrical charge found in the liquid part of the blood. Electrolytes are important for the health of the pet and are involved in many aspects of body function- including the heart, and muscle, and nerve action.

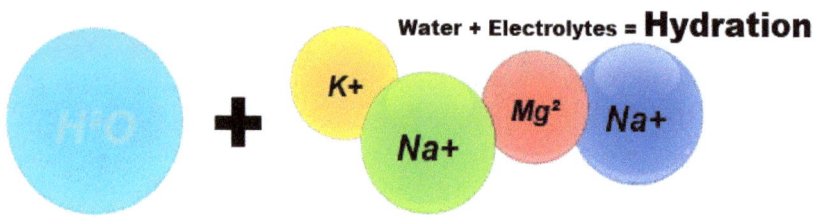

Some electrolytes are:

- sodium
- chloride
- potassium
- calcium
- magnesium
- and many others

PANCREATIC TESTING

The pancreas is an organ that has many jobs, one of which is to help break down food.

The pancreas makes chemicals (enzymes) that break down proteins, sugars, and fats into very small particles that can be absorbed and used by the body. If the pancreas is irritated- sometimes by fatty foods or diseases- then it becomes painful and pancreatitis occurs. Pets with pancreatitis may have the following signs:

- pain the abdomen
- vomiting
- diarrhea- with blood sometimes
- decreased or no appetite
- depression
- or other changes in the cat's condition

FPL-(Feline pancreatic lipase) is a separate and special test utilized to specifically identify pancreatitis.

Pancreatitis is a very serious condition and treatment is always recommended.

THYROID TESTING

Thyroid glands are glands located along both sides of the windpipe (trachea) in the neck of the cat.

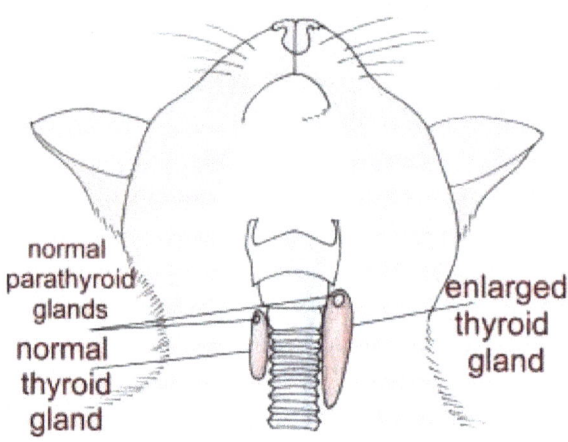

Thyroid glands make thyroid hormone - a hormone essential for the cat's health.

While dogs may have disorders where too little thyroid hormone, cats generally have disorders where too much thyroid hormone is made by their thyroid glands. This is called hyperthyroidism (hyper- high, thyroidism- relating to the thyroid).

Some signs of increased thyroid hormone disorder in the cat include:

- symptoms in many organ systems due to the overall increase in metabolism
- weight loss
- increased appetite
- unkempt appearance
- poor body condition
- vomiting
- diarrhea
- increased thirst (polydipsia)
- increased urine (polyuria)
- rapid breathing (tachypnea)
- difficulty breathing (dyspnea)
- heart murmur or fast or irregular heart rate – sometimes a "gallop rhythm"
- hyperactivity
- aggression
- enlarged thyroid gland, which can be felt as a lump on the neck
- thickened nails

Several tests are available for evaluating thyroid disorders, however, the Total Thyroxine- T4- is the level most commonly evaluated.

When T4 levels are high, several treatments are available. Some include:
- daily administration of medication that reduces the production of thyroid hormone – these are effective and inexpensive, however, require lifelong administration and may have side effects when given for a long time
- radioactive iodine can be injected into a cat that results in the destruction of the thyroid cells – this is safe and effective, however more expensive and requires hospitalization in a specialty clinic
- diet- a new diet- Y/D has been developed for cats with over functioning thyroid glands- this food has low levels of Iodine- which is necessary to make the thyroid hormone and if Iodine is not available, then a cat cannot make too much hormone. This is effective, but may be difficult in homes with other cats- the other cats may have the diet, however, they need salt with Iodine added to their diets to remain healthy
- surgical removal of the thyroid glands is also available- this is costly and requires hormone replacement afterwards for the life of the cat

Pets given medication for hyperthyroid condition, or who are fed Y/D, require regular evaluations of the levels of T4 assure the T4 levels are within the 'normal' range for evaluation of therapy. As with any treatment, the T4 levels that are initially too high can become too low.

Medication adjustments are made depending on whether the T4 levels become too low with treatment or have not decreased sufficiently with treatment.

The goal of therapy is to maintain the level of T4 hormone in a 'normal' range. Testing makes this possible.

BUN and CREATININE

Creatinine (kree – at – in- inn) - is a product of muscle breakdown, and is usually produced at a fairly constant rate by the body (depending on muscle mass) – it is eliminated by the kidneys.

Blood urea nitrogen (BUN) (blood - your- ee- ah- nigh- tro- gen) – is a test that measures the amount of nitrogen in the cat's blood that comes from the breakdown of proteins - BUN is made in the liver and eliminated by the kidneys in the urine.

Both creatinine and BUN tests are completed to evaluate how well a cat's kidneys are functioning.

When these two levels are elevated, a diagnosis of kidney failure may be considered. Other tests may be recommended to make certain there are no other reasons for these elevations.

Cat's with kidney failure may also develop elevated phosphorous levels in their blood, may become anemic, may develop high blood pressure and may have decreased urine concentrations- (known as the specific gravity of the urine).

New testing is coming to detect kidney disorders earlier than we can with the BUN and creatinine

Causes of kidney failure include:

1. advancing age
2. disorders of the kidneys from birth
3. blockage of the urinary system
4. certain medications
5. cancer
6. diabetes

Symptoms often occur gradually over an extended period. In addition, symptoms may vary and not all of these listed below will be seen in every cat:

- increase in water intake in the early phases
- increase in urination in the early phases
- loss of appetite in later phases
- sluggishness in later phases
- vomiting as failure progresses
- diarrhea or constipation
- depression
- weight loss
- high blood pressure
- pale gums- from anemia
- in severe failure- blindness, seizures, coma

DIABETIC TESTING

Diabetes mellitus is a disorder of a cat's ability to properly use sugar.

Most cats with diabetes require insulin daily.

Cats also require a special diet to assist in controlling their blood sugars.

Cats require close monitoring of the effects of the insulin as well.

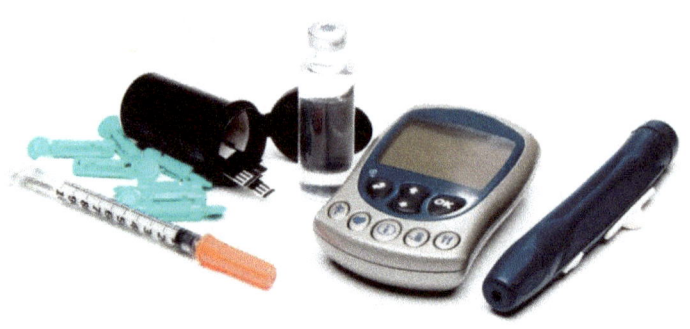

Accucheck- is a test with a small machine that uses one drop of blood to quickly measure the sugar (glucose) in the blood.

Blood glucose- a test in a veterinarian office or a laboratory to test for the level of sugar (glucose) in the cat's blood. A larger amount of blood is required to complete this test and may be completed with other lab testing.

Glucose curve- is a series of sugar (glucose) measurements after a cat is given insulin- usually every 1-2 hours. This testing is useful in adjusting the dosage of medication (insulin) being given to a diabetic cat because it documents the sugar changes over time after the pet is given insulin.

Fructosamine – a measurement of the sugar in a cat's blood over a long period of time. This test is useful in evaluating the effective use of insulin in treating diabetes. This is a more effective measurement of the treatment of diabetes in cats because cats tend to become very frightened in a veterinary office and when this occurs, their sugar increases dramatically. This may confuse evaluation of the result and the treatment effectiveness. This frightened response does not alter a fructosamine test.

HEARTWORMS

Heartworm is a disease that has been more commonly associated with dogs; however, cats can be infected with heartworms as well. Outdoor cats are more at risk than indoor cats.

Heartworm is also known as Dirofilariasis in cats because is caused by infestation of the organism *Dirofilaria immitis*. This worm is commonly referred to as the heartworm.

Heartworms are spread through mosquito bites carrying infective heartworm larvae.

The lifecycle of heartworms affecting cats is shorter than the cycle of those infecting dogs.

It is important to note that the presence of microfilaria- offspring of the adult worms- in the blood is in fact *uncommon* in cats, and has been seen in less than 20 percent of infected cats.

The severity of this disease in cats is depends on:
- the number of heartworms present
- how long the cat has been infected
- the response of the cat to the heartworms

Signs of heartworm in cats include:
- coughing
- difficulty or noisy breathing (may resemble asthma)
- vomiting
- depression
- sometimes a murmur can be heard by the veterinarian
- sometimes an infected cat can have an irregular heart rate
- decreased or no appetite
- weight loss

In severe cases, a cat may:
- have difficulty walking
- have seizures
- faint or collapse
- have fluid in their abdomen
- become suddenly blind
- loss of pet is possible

As can be seen, these signs are vague and can be attributed to many disorders in cats.

HEARTWORM IS A PREVENTABLE DISEASE

The GOAL in heartworm prevention is to eliminate immature larvae stages in the skin before they are able to mature into adult worms that travel to the heart.

This goal is accomplished by breaking the cycle of the heartworm infection with medication that kills any larvae that may be deposited in your pet's skin.

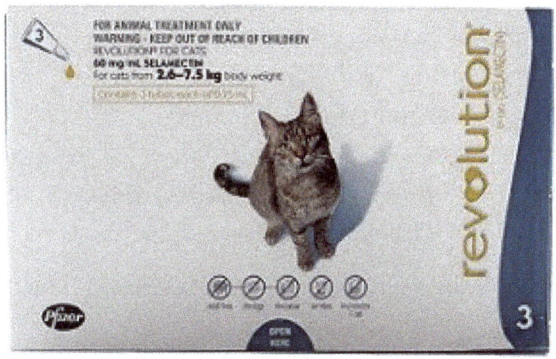

Revolution shown above and Advantage Muti and Heartguard are two additional products effective for preventing heartworm disease in cats.

Since heartworm microfliaria are microscopic and cannot be seen in a cat's skin, it is recommended that all cats over 8 weeks old be on heartworm prevention all year and be tested regularly for heartworm disease.

Reasons to Prevent Heartworm Disease

Reasons heartworm prevention is recommended for all cats are:

- it is more difficult to diagnose heartworm disease in cats than dogs
- it is not known how many cats have heartworm disease because cats are not generally tested for this disease yearly as dogs are
- there is no treatment for heartworm disease in cats – only dog treatment is available
- prevention is safe and easy
- cats may die suddenly from the disease and it can take up to 2-3 years for this disease to be eliminated in an infected cat

FELINE LEUKEMIA/FELINE IMMUNODEFICIENCY VIRUS/HEARTWORM TESTING

Simple testing is available for the serious diseases of leukemia, immunodeficiency virus, and heartworms. Testing is done by drawing a blood sample and completing a special test – one such combination test is noted above.

HEPATIC LIPIDOSIS

HEPATIC LIPIDOSIS (hep- attic- lip-id-oh-sis) – is also known as fatty liver disease.

This condition occurs when fat accumulates in the liver cells. The fat deposited in the liver can severely impair the health and proper functioning of the liver and, if not treated, can lead to the loss of the cat.

Reasons for Fat Deposition in the Liver

The most common reason for fat to deposit in the liver of a cat is loss of appetite. It is a very serious concern when a cat does not eat. Any reason for the lack of appetite leads to fat depositing in the liver. This is because when the cat does not eat, they begin to break down the fats in their body to use as sugar for energy. It is this break down of excess fats that leads to the fatty liver disorder described here.

Underlying reasons for hepatic lipidosis to develop also include:

1. obesity
2. diabetes
3. cancer
4. hyperthyroidism
5. pancreatitis
6. kidney disease
7. any type of liver problem
8. any reason a cat stops eating may lead to hepatic lipidosis - a cat that is not eating needs veterinary care

Signs of fatty liver disease in cats include:

- decrease in their appetite- they may stop eating altogether
- hiding – being away from their owner
- weakness
- jaundice- a yellow coloring to the whites of the eyes, the gums or skin in the inside of the ears
- drooling- which can be one sign of nausea
- vomiting
- constipation
- weight loss
- dehydration
- enlargement of the liver- which may be felt when the veterinarian examines the cat's abdomen or seen on x-rays or an ultrasound exam

If not treated, signs of liver failure include:

- black, tarry stools
- bruising in the skin
- coma
- seizures
- loss of the pet

Treatment for fatty liver disease has better results when started early and includes intravenous fluids and sugar as well as constant monitoring to reverse the fat deposits in the liver to save the cat.

XRAYS

Radiographs- AKA- x-rays- are useful in identifying broken bones, arthritis, obstructions in a cat's intestines, constipation, heart size, enlarged organs, stones in bladders, screening lung health, and sometimes other uses.

ULTRASOUND

Ultrasound is a non invasive test without radiation available for more detailed imaging of body organs such as the heart, liver, kidneys, pancreas, eyes, lymph nodes, testicles, ovaries and uterus, kittens in pregnant moms, intestines, spleen, stones in bladders, and so forth.

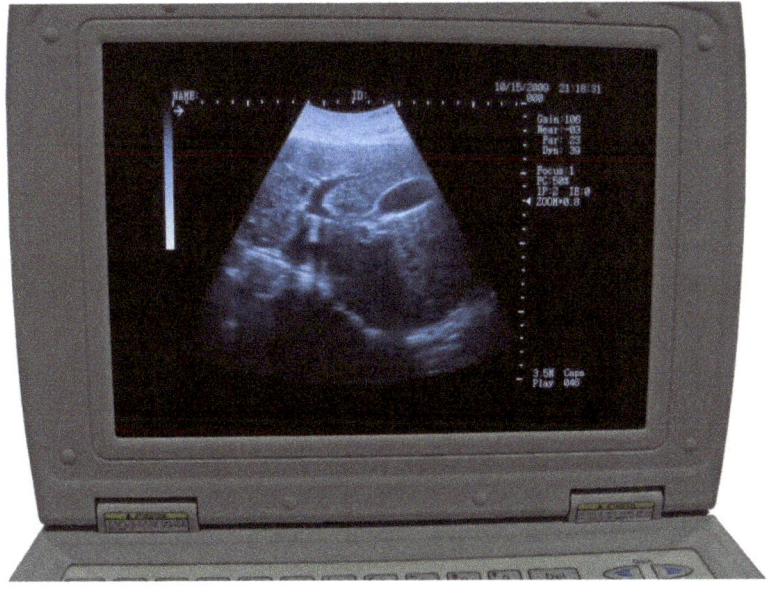

Some veterinarians are skilled at this technique and some advise referral to specialists for this testing

ADVANCED IMAGING

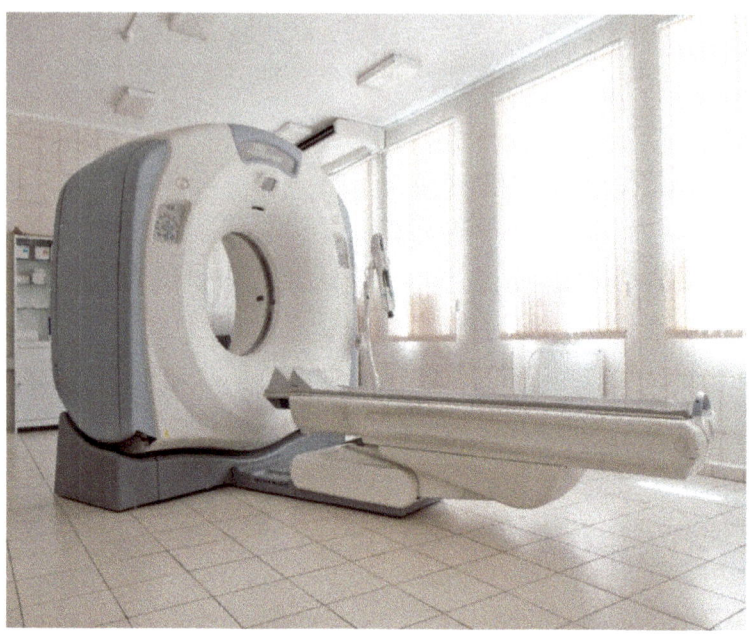

More advanced imaging has been developed. This includes the CT scan (computerized topography) and the MRI (magnetic resonance imaging). These tests are more accurate and quicker at assisting veterinarians find and treat disorders affecting cats.

SKIN TESTING

Owners frequently present with concerns about skin. Some of these include:

- itching and scratching
- flaking skin
- excessive licking of the legs/paws/any body area
- hair loss
- infections- abscesses with drainage that may have an odor
- open bleeding areas of the skin
- growths in the skin
- odor to the skin
- oily skin
- fleas
- and other symptoms

Skin Disorders

POSSIBLE DISORDERS OF THE SKIN INCLUDE:

1. **Immune** - mediated diseases- which include skin allergies to fleas most often, but also to grass/pollens/molds. etc, mites, and yeast infections
2. **Ear mites**- are included in the section on ears, but are also considered a skin disorder since the skin of the ear is a continuation of the skin of the rest of the body
3. **Skin mites**- Notoedres mites is the most commonly seen mite as well as Cheyletialla mites are possible infestations of the cat/kitten skin
4. **Physical/environmental conditions**- which included 'hot spots and lick irritations
5. **Infections**- with any bacteria or yeast- one example is staph- a normal bacteria found on the skin- and other is malassezia- a normal fungi (yeast) found on the skin
6. **Ringworm**- is also considered an infectious condition of the skin- caused by a fungi that grows on the skin
7. **Fleas and ticks** – can be seen on cats and kittens skin
8. **Hereditary conditions** - which includes seborrhea- too much oil made by the skin, pattern baldness, color dilution
9. **Symptoms** of skin disease may be related to conditions occurring inside the body- such as a high functioning thyroid or diabetes or kidney disease
10. **Tumors**- also included are cancers in the skin

Just to name a few conditions veterinarians must consider when presented with skin concerns

Skin tests include:

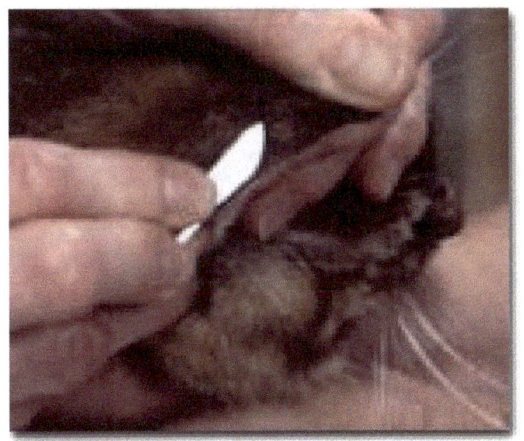

- skin scraping
- skin biopsy
- skin impressions
- cultures of the skin – for bacterial and fungal infection
- ear swabs – for mites or infection of the ears

Skin is easy to test because it is accessible to a veterinarian.

SKIN SCRAPE

A skin scrape is where a sharp blade is used to scrape affected areas of skin to place on a microscope slide to view the scraping under the microscope.

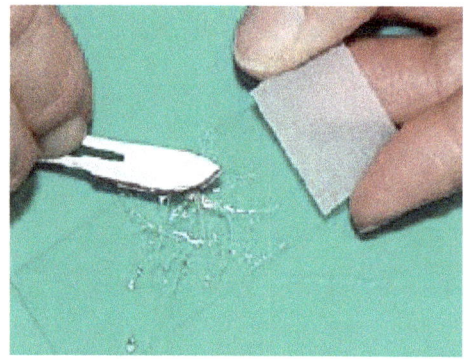

Veterinarians recommend skin scraping to detect Notoedric mites – scabies in cats/kittens

Notoedric mites are mites that burrow into the skin of affected pets

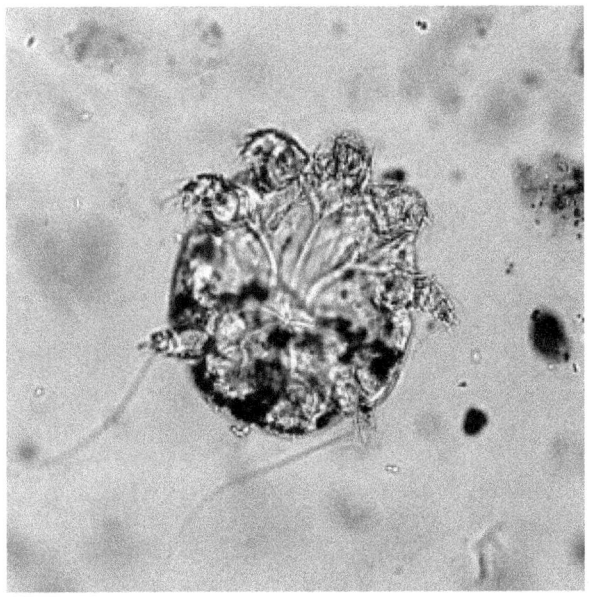

Some signs of notoedric mites include:

1. intense itching and scratching
2. hair loss- that can be extreme
3. red bumps
4. red skin- open sores
5. depression
6. loss of appetite due to being so uncomfortable resulting in
7. weight loss and ...
8. loss of pet is possible if not treated

If owners are in close contact with an infected pet, they may be at risk for these mites to burrow in their skin and cause intense itching; however, humans are considered a temporary host for the mite.

Several treatments are available to treat Notoedric mites

FLEAS

Many pets have fleas in their fur; however, some cats have a reaction to them. These cats have a flea allergy. Signs of flea allergy include-

- itching and scratching
- hair loss
- sores on the cat's body
- loss of appetite
- infection of the skin

Recommended treatment for fleas includes:

- treating all pets in the home all year
- cleaning all surfaces and bedding related to the pet in the home
- treating the environment if possible (the yard)

Cats allergic to fleas may require additional medication to ease the intense itching and scratching they experience when exposed to fleas.

CULTURES

Cultures are samples taken of fluids or tissues that are then placed on special gel plates so bacteria or fungi can grow and be identified.

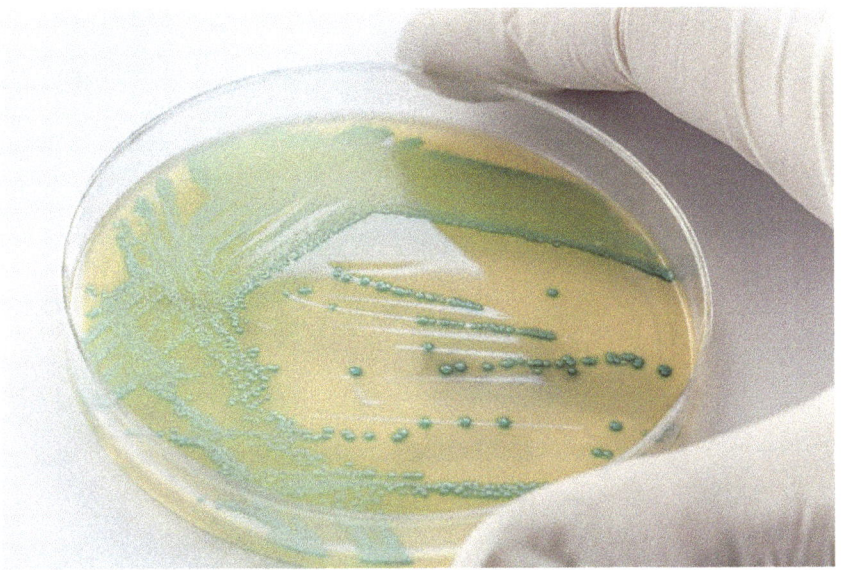

Fluids commonly cultured are:

- blood
- urine
- wound fluids
- skin
- ears

Cultures are usually recommended when infections are severe or are not improving with treatment.

RINGWORM

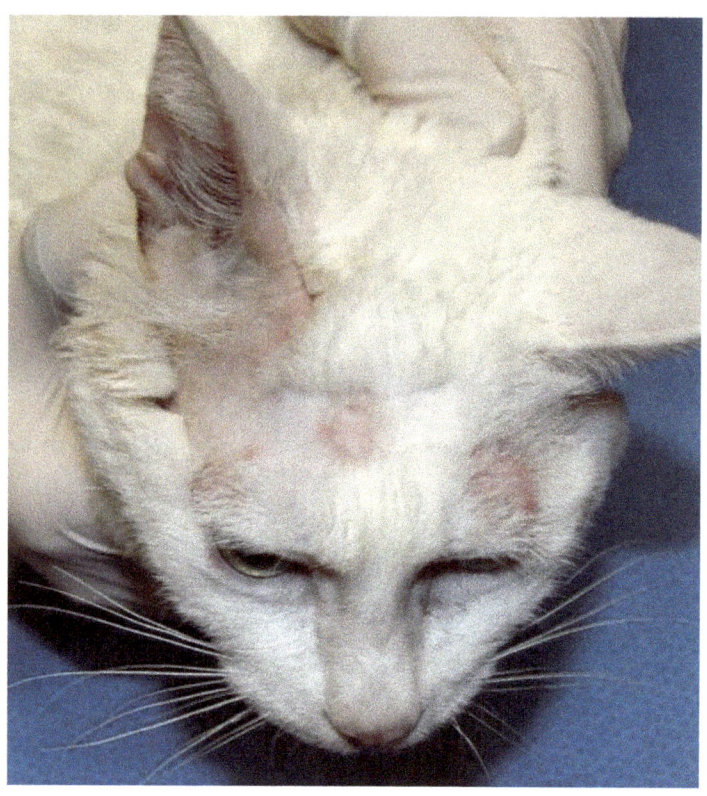

Ringworm is not a worm but is a common fungal infection of the skin. Ringworm can grow on any part of the skin, however, is mostly seen on the face and the legs. The areas infected are usually circular- ring-like.

Ringworm may be spred to people. Always take care when handling and treating new cats or kittens because humans can acquire ringworm when exposed to the infection.

FUNGAL CULTURES

DTM (dermatophyte (derr- mat- oh- fight-) test media) - is a special culture gel used to detect fungal infections.

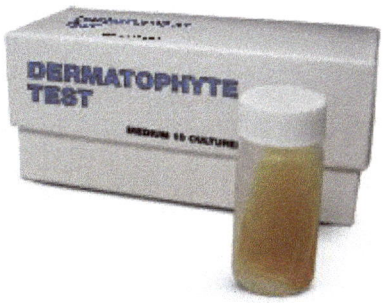

Your veterinarian may recommend testing for this infection.

FELINE ACNE

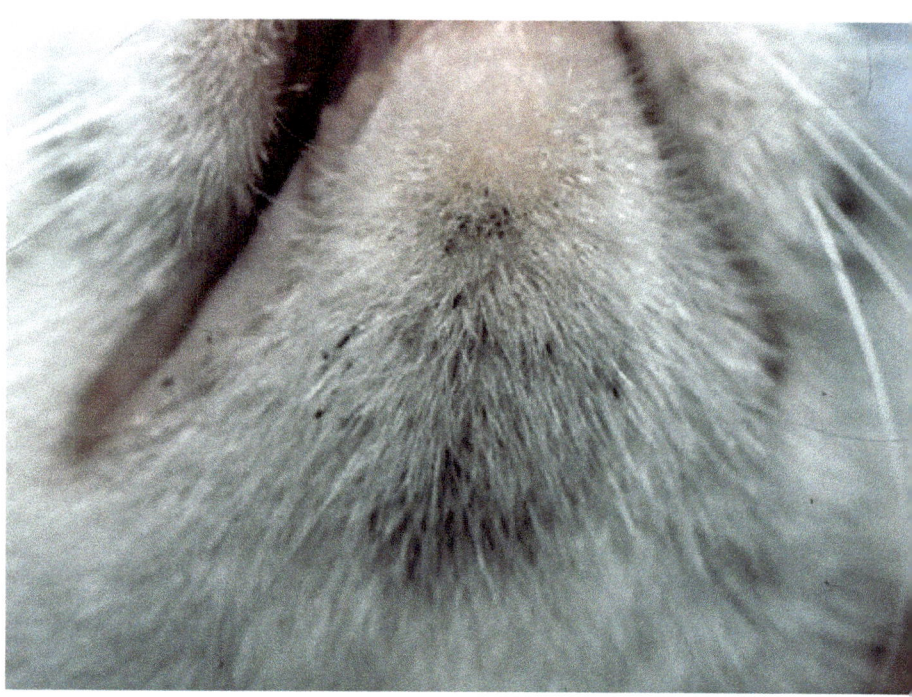

Feline acne is a common infection in the skin of the chin of the cat.

Tests such as cultures can be performed to confirm the presence of acne, however, most veterinarians are able to provided treatment after inspecting the cat's chin area.

URINE EXAMS

Owners present with concerns relating to urinary disorders in cats that include:

1. blood in urine- sometimes seen as 'red tinged' urine
2. inability to urinate- which is an emergency
3. urinating frequently
4. urinating small amounts of urine
5. urinating large amounts of urine
6. urine with a strong or foul odor
7. seeing stones passed in urine
8. crying with pain

Some disorders of the urinary system in cats include:

1. infection
2. diseases such as diabetes or liver or other organ disorders
3. tumors (cancer)
4. stones (calculi)
5. crystals- several different types may be found – one type in particular is pictured on page 238

Urine test - the urinalysis- is recommended when owners have concerns or as routine screening test

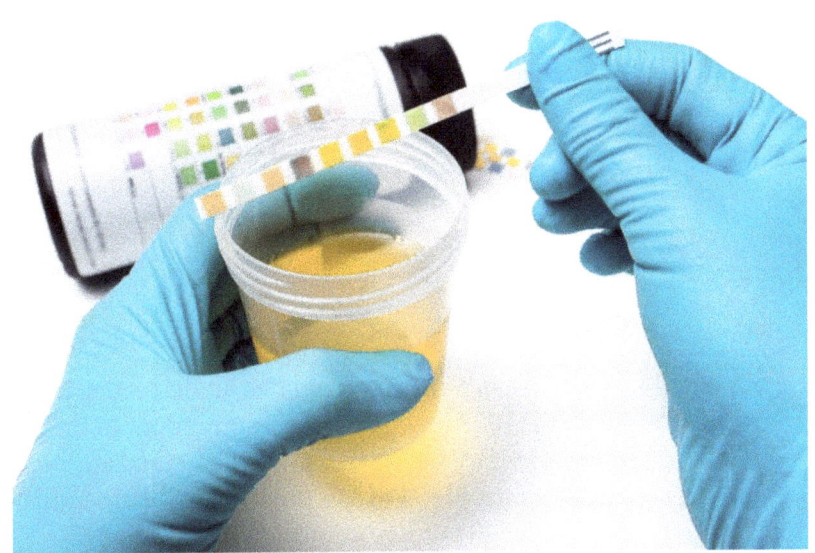

The 3 parts to a urine exam are:

1. specific gravity- measures urine concentration
2. the 'strip' portion- screens for protein, blood, white blood cells, sugar, and other items in the urine.
3. the 'microscopic' portion- examines stained slides for crystals, red and white blood cells, tumor cells, and other potential findings.

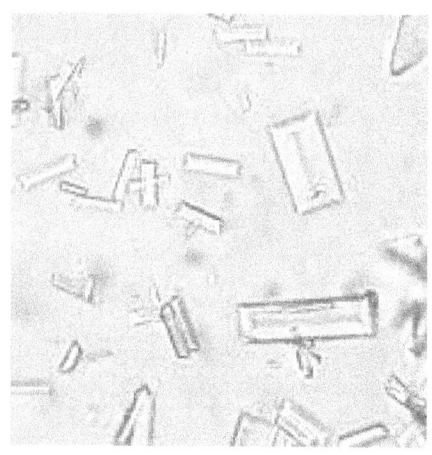

Crystals (above) found in urine samples indicate the presence of these crystals in the bladder and these are important to find and treat because they can lead to stones made of the crystals. Stones or the crystals themselves may lead to life threatening bladder obstruction (below) - this condition is more common in male cats.

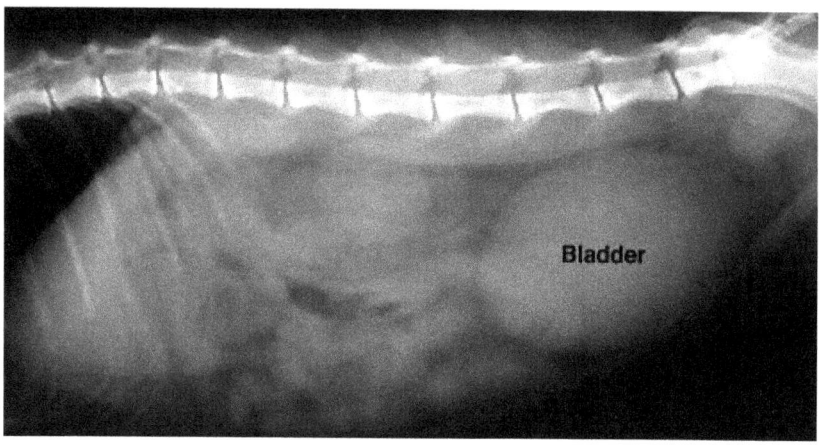

EARS

Owners frequently seek veterinarian care for problems relating to ears that include:

1. scratching or rubbing the ears
2. crying when the ears are touched or massaged
3. odor from the ears
4. discharge from the ears- brown, green, or yellow for example
5. tilting of the pet's head
6. growths noticed in or around the ears
7. circling
8. loss of balance
9. sores to the ear flap
10. shaking their head
11. hair loss around the ear
12. swelling or redness to the ears
13. and possibly hearing loss

Veterinarians examine a cat's ear canal and ear drum with an oto - (ear) scope

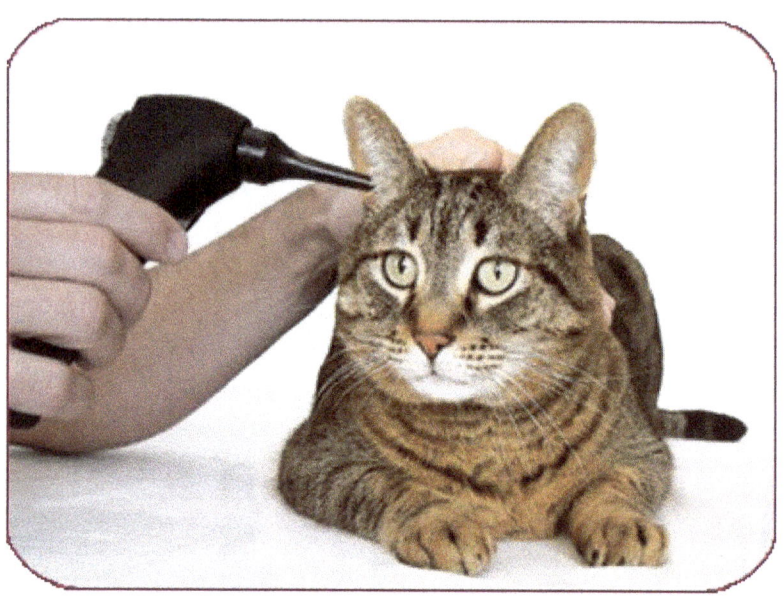

When discharge is present in the ears of a cat, an ear swab exam may be recommended

Ear swabs help direct the care recommended for ear disorders and are completed by-

- using a q- tip to obtain a sample of the ear discharge from the ear canals
- this discharge is placed on a slide
- then stained
- then examined for yeast and bacteria

For ear health, veterinarians recommend:

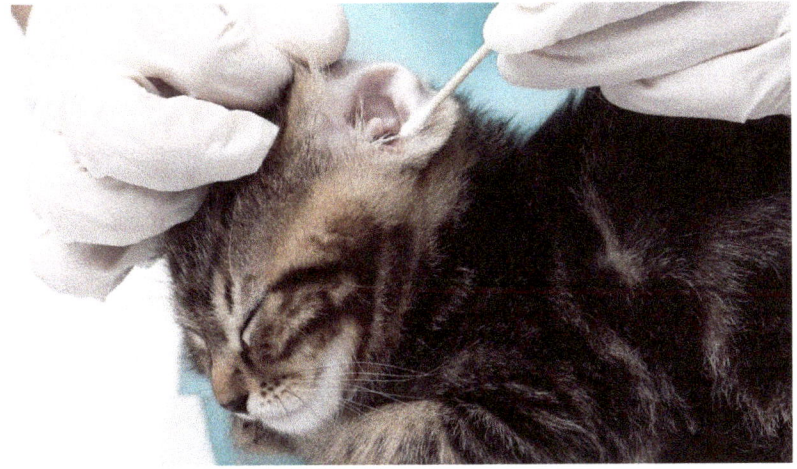

1. cleaning the ears if there is discharge
2. using medication recommended by your veterinarian
3. cleaning the ears after bathing and swimming
4. treating all known diseases- such as allergies/diabetes/others
5. having the ears checked regularly

EAR MITES

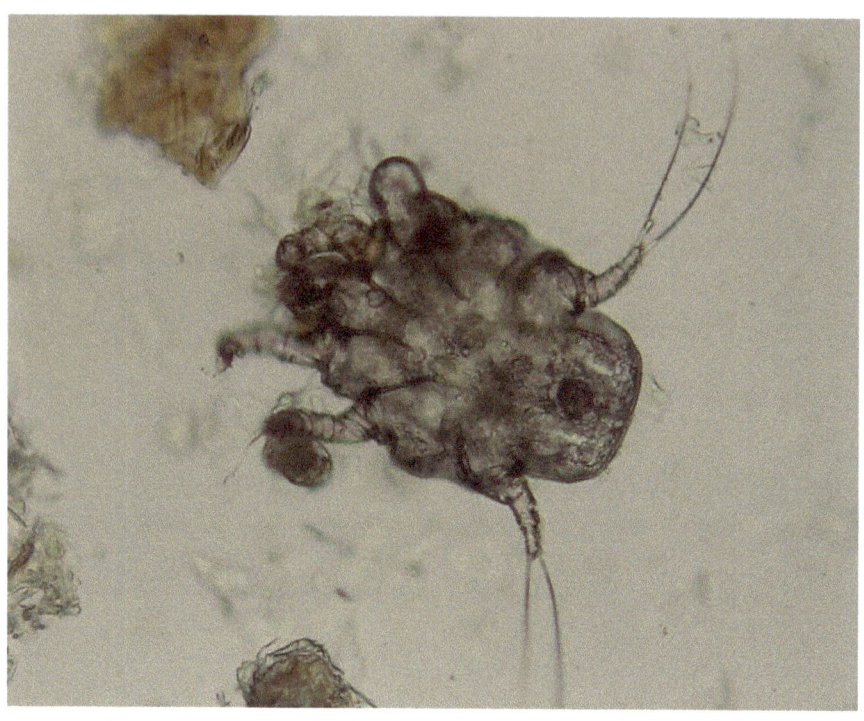

Ear mites are common in young kittens. It you see black discharge or your kitten is itching and scratching at their ears, it is recommended to look for mites.

Treatment is simple and your veterinarian will be able to make recommendations.

EYES

Owners frequently seek veterinarian care for concerns relating to eyes which include:

1. excessive tearing
2. squinting
3. swelling of the eye or eyelids
4. reddening to the eyelids
5. cloudiness inside or on the surface of the eye
6. colored discharge (white, tan, green, yellow) around the eye
7. pain
8. unequal pupil size
9. bleeding from the eye or inside the eye
10. injury to the eye- from being hit, bitten, scratched,
11. inability to see

Disorders of the eyes in cats include:

- infection- including conjunctivitis
- disorders of the cornea (the clear surface of the eye)-including ulcers
- disorders of the lens (including cataracts)
- foreign objects in the eye
- cuts to the eye or eyelids
- trauma – an injury to the eye
- tumors
- glaucoma
- blindness
- and more

Veterinarians examine the cat's eye with an ophthalmoscope – to visualize deep and superficial areas of the eye

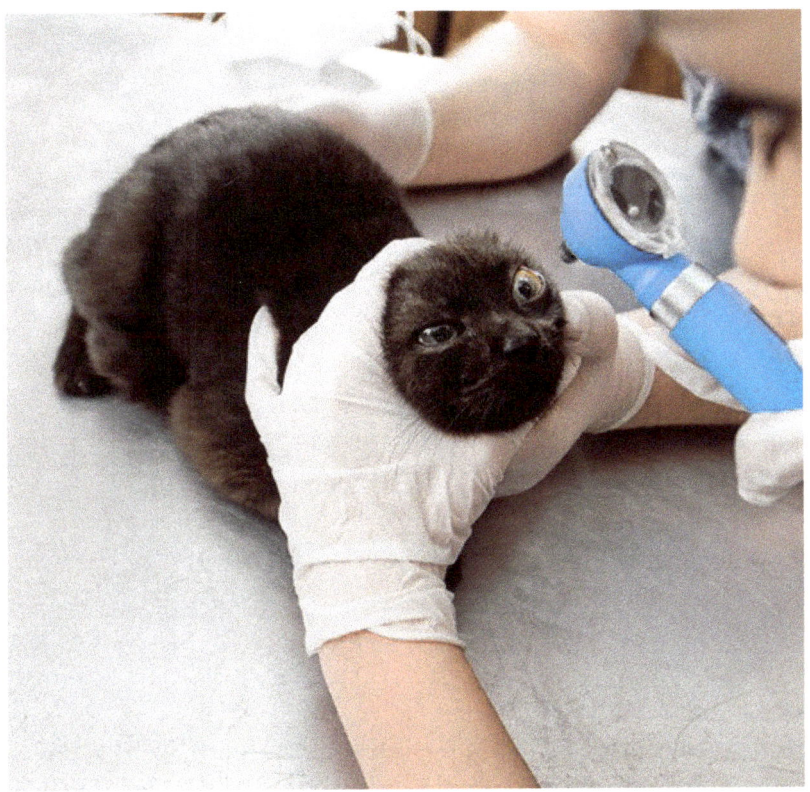

Specialists are available for severe disorders of the eye

Three tests commonly used to evaluate cats' eyes are:

EYE STAINING

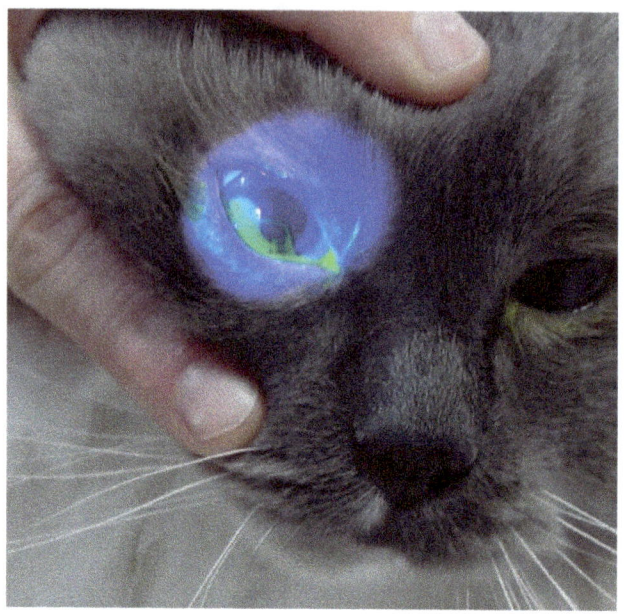

Fluorescein stain- a liquid green dye applied to the surface of the eye to detect superficial defects on the surface of the eye. If a defect is present, the stain will dye this area a green color.

TEAR TESTING

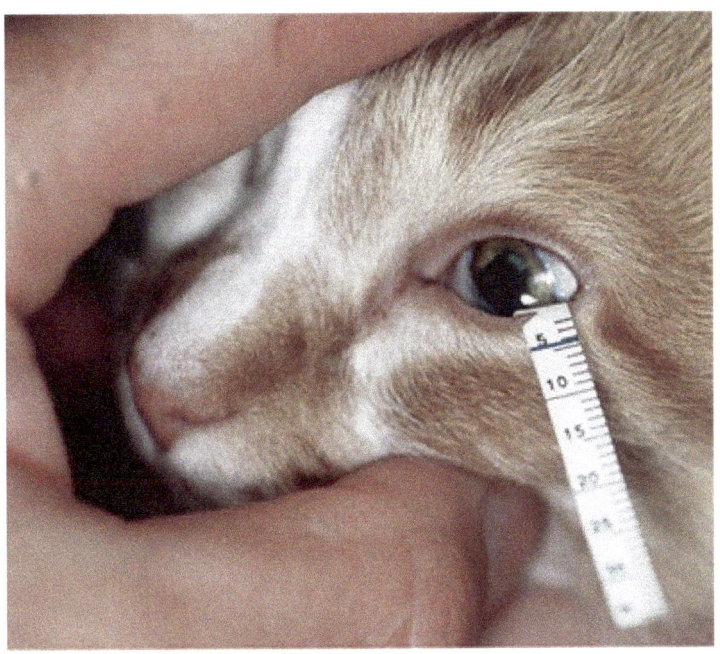

Tear testing - in which a small piece of special paper with measurement lines is inserted into the lower eyelid for one minute and the amount of liquid tears present on the paper is measured.

Healthy eyes constantly make tears that are spread over the eyes each time a pet blinks. Tears keep the eyes moist and clean.

When too many tears are made, they spill over onto the fur of the face- a condition called epiphora.

When there is a condition where too little tears are made, this is known as dry eye' (keratoconjunctivitis sicca). This condition requires treatment to keep the eye/s that are affected healthy.

TONOMETRY

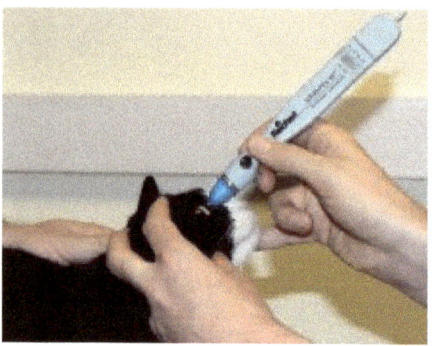

A tonometer- or tono pen – as seen above, measures the pressure in the eye.

This test is to screen for glaucoma. Glaucoma is present when eye pressures are high (elevated.) Glaucoma can be very painful and can cause loss of vision. This test helps determine if a cat requires treatment for this condition.

BARTONELLA -CAT SCRATCH FEVER

Bartonella- (bar-ton-ell-ah) - Bartonellosis (bar- ton- ell- oh- sis) - is known as cat scratch disease or cat scratch fever.

This is an emerging disease worldwide that is most commonly caused in cats by *Bartonella henselae* bacteria.

Cats who acquire bartonellosis can transmit this disease to humans. When a disease can be transmitted to humans it is called a zoonotic disease. Cats can transmit *Bartonella* bacteria to people through scratches and bites.

Signs of Bartonella include:

- no symptoms of illness at all
- mild, non - specific symptoms like fever, tired
- lack of appetite

However, more severe symptoms that may be seen include:
- deep eye infection
- enlarged lymph nodes
- muscle pain
- inability to have kittens
- irritation of the heart
- kittens may have any body area affected

It is important to seek veterinary care for cats that are ill.

HAIRBALLS

Hairballs in cats are called trichobezoars (trike-oh-beez-oars). Tricho- means 'hair' and bezoar – means a mass trapped in the stomach and intestines.

Cats obtain hairballs from licking their coats as they groom themselves. The cat swallows the hair. This hair accumulates in their stomach and when it becomes a 'ball,' the cat vomits to remove it.

If hair is allowed to pass from the stomach into the intestines, it slows the travel of the food and hair through the intestines, more water is absorbed from the passing material, and this results in a more constipated stool.

We all know hair balls

1. are unpleasant for the pet and the owner – especially if the cat retches to remove the hair
2. are unpleasant to clean up
3. may cause intestinal blockage and constipation
4. may cause lack of appetite or decreased nutrition from vomiting food- resulting in weight loss and malnutrition
5. are more common in long haired cats, but are potential and present in all cats
6. can confuse owners for more serious causes of vomiting and lack of appetite

Hairballs can be prevented by using hair ball products regularly and brushing cats/kittens.

As stated, hairballs can result in constipation. Seen below is an x-ray of a cat with...

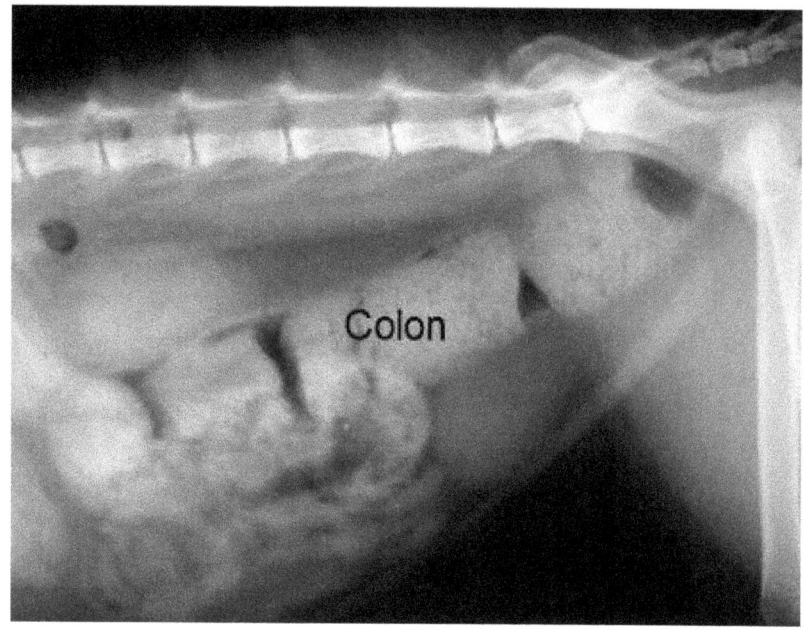

......constipation.

The difficulty when cats become constipated, is they stop eating- which may lead to serious disorders covered earlier in this chapter- and they may be unable to pass the fecal material at all. This sometimes leads to the need for enemas and veterinary care.

Constipation is easy to prevent with the use of hairball medication because the hairball medication not only prevents hairballs, it acts as a laxative.

The BENEFITS of testing are that it allows veterinarians the best practice options....

… to keep pets healthy and happy!

Chapter 13
MISCELLANEOUS

LOST PETS

Many owners find themselves in the unfortunate position of having lost a cat

- every few seconds a lost cat is taken to an animal shelter
- we want you to be one of the families reunited with their lost pet

Some helpful recommendations for finding a lost cat are:

- **act immediately-** the quicker a search is started, the more likely the lost cat may be found
- **utilize web sources** – there are several on line sources for posting or checking for lost cats
- **check local pet shelters** – know all the local shelters in your immediate area and several surrounding areas- it is possible for cats to travel distances when lost
- **contact animal control agencies** – know all the local authorities and their policies regarding lost cats
- **call local papers** – some papers have special areas in the paper to post lost and/or found pets
- **call micro chipping services-** if your cat is micro chipped, call to ask if any reported animals have been found and also advise them of your lost pet
- **LOOK everywhere-** in your neighborhood and in surrounding neighborhoods and everywhere in your home
- **visit local businesses-** they may allow you to post signs or someone may have seen the cat while coming to work
- **talk to letter carriers-** who are in the neighborhood and can keep an eye out or may have seen your cat
- **talk to neighbors**
- **talk to the paper delivery person**
- **talk to the garbage collector**
- **ask children in the neighborhood**
- **ADVERTISE** a reward, however, consider not posting the amount of the reward
- **post signs** up in neighborhood
- **microchip** your cat
- **attach** a name tag and phone number to a collar of your cat
- **do not give up**

MICROCHIPPING

Micro chipping is a small cylinder (about the size of a grain of rice) that is injected beneath a cat's skin- usually in the area between the shoulders. With active cats, the chip may move slightly from the original site of insertion.

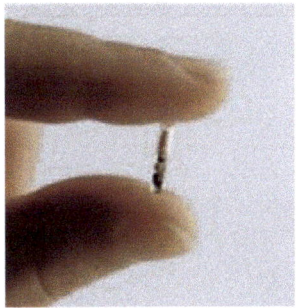

Each cylinder has a number that is unique and identifies the cat it is inserted into.

The chips are scanned with a special scanner that connects information to owners.

There are national and international chips available if you plan to travel abroad with a cat.

EMERGENCIES

Emergencies happen to cats. Being prepared helps during these stressful times.

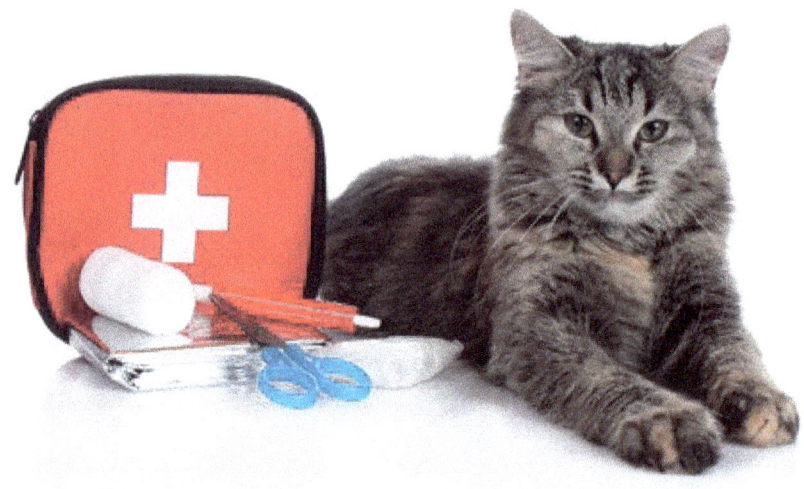

Common cat emergencies include:

- being hit by a car
- poisoning
- broken bones
- objects stuck in the intestine (strings, toys, etc)
- overheating in automobiles or in warm environments
- low body temperature if out in cold environments
- snake bites
- other animal bites – which may result in infection/abscesses/and possibly disease
- bleeding from anybody area
- eye injuries
- being unable to urinate
- reactions to vaccines or medications
- seizures (particularly if they do not stop or the pet has several in succession)
- sudden collapse
- any sudden change in a pet's condition

WHAT TO DO:

- be prepared - have supplies and know all the emergency clinic and personal veterinary clinic phone numbers in your area
- know any dangers in the world around you - weather, snakes, plants, animals, and more
- begin transferring the pet to a veterinary clinic as soon as possible
- while seeking veterinary care, have someone drive you if possible

HOW TO CHECK VITAL SIGNS:

Vital Signs Are- Heart Rate, Breathing (respiratory) Rate, Temperature

Heart rate- normal is 140-220 beats per minute - pain and fear may make the rate higher - to check a cat's heart rate- place your hand over the chest- it is easiest over the left side of the chest behind the left front leg- another way to check a pulse is to slip your hand under rear leg into the groin to feel a pulse-owners can be shown- measure 15 seconds and x 4

Breathing (respiratory) rate –normal is 24-42 breaths per minute - pain and fear may make the rate higher -to check a cat's respiratory rate- observe chest rising and, if you know how, listen with a stethoscope –owners can be shown - measure 15 seconds and x by 4

Temperature – normal is 100-102.5 F - to check the temperature, always use a rectal digital thermometer

Abnormal temperatures are if < 100 F or > 103 F

Never be afraid to ask someone to show you how to check your pet

Seek veterinary care immediately and-

STAY CALM

- do not put your face or a child's face by the injured cat's face- they may bite or scratch if fearful or painful even if they would not under normal circumstances
- if the cat is overheated, begin to cool pet off by placing the cat in a shaded area with a fan- if T > 104- seek a VETERINARIAN immediately and use tepid water baths and isopropyl rubbing alcohol to the cat's foot pads – this may help lower the temperature
- wrap cold cats in warm blankets – but do not rub areas that may be frostbitten
- wrap injured cats or kittens in towels for transport

ALSO:

- protect injured legs or broken legs – rescuers can use rolled up towels to protect or immobilize an injured leg by placing the towel next to the injured legs to act as splints or supports- this helps the injured part stay still while the cat is transported to the veterinary clinic
- cats are small enough to be transferred safely on small blankets, rugs, or towels
- take any poisons or medications the cat has ingested
- use soft bandages for open wounds or bleeding – apply gentle pressure to bleeding areas – you may need to keep gentle pressure until the bleeding stops or you arrive at the veterinary clinic

Items to Include in a Home First Aid Kit:

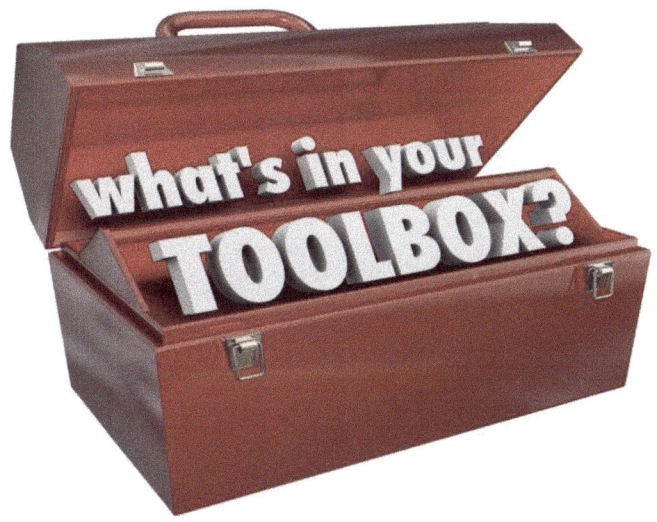

- alcohol (70% isopropyl alcohol-rubbing alcohol)
- antibacterial cream
- bandaging material- gauze pads, gauze rolls, rolls of cotton, self adhesive wraps such as 'vet wrap' or 'co flex' bandage
- cotton balls
- hydrogen peroxide
- rectal thermometer
- scissors
- blankets and towels
- tweezers
- the phone numbers to the local emergency clinics
- the phone number to poison control

Keep the kit in a sealed container in your home and/or vehicle.

Examining your pet

Knowing what a normal exam is for your pet makes it easier to know when veterinary care is needed.

Basic Physical Exam is from head to toe -

First- before starting an exam- look at your cat in general- are they awake, happy to see you, moving correctly? How are they standing and breathing? Acting normal? In good spirits?

Normal: awake and playful, responding when called, walking correctly, breathing easily
Not Normal: will not wake up for you, unable to stand, breathing heavily, anything that concerns you

Head: look at the pet's head area

Normal: rounded forehead, smooth hair coat, no missing hair, no bumps
Not Normal: open wounds, bumps or swelling in the head area, shape of the head not the same on both sides

Eyes: look at both eyes

Normal: bright, moist, clear, equal pupils, whites of eyes white in color, look the same on both sides, looks at you when you are talking
Not normal: dull, sunken eyes that appear dry or cloudy, colored discharge from the eyes, yellow or red color to the whites of the eyes, squinting, swelling, painful appearance to the eyes, crying when attempting to open the eyelids

Ears: look at both ears

Normal: pale pink, no odor, dry, typical carriage of ears
Not Normal: swelling to any area of the ear, odor, redness, pain, wounds, scabs, rash, not carrying ears the same on both sides- for example- one up, one down

(Continued assessment of the head areas)

Nose: look at the nose

Normal: moist and clean
Not Normal: very dry and cracked, colored discharge- white, green, yellow, tan, red, bleeding, swelling, loss of pigment (coloring) of the nose

Throat: look at the throat and gently feel the throat as well

Normal: no cough, no swellings or growths, all areas feel the same on both sides of the neck
Not Normal: cough when gently feeling the neck area, difficulties in breathing, swelling, growths, anything that feels larger on one side than the other

Oral- look at the cat's teeth and open mouth by turning up the lip fold

Normal: teeth are clean and white, the gums are pink and not overgrown
Not Normal: tartar on teeth, recession of gums, reddening of the gums, odor to the mouth or green/tan/yellow discharge from the gums around any teeth, sores in the mouth, growths in the mouth, excess gums over the teeth

MM- the mucous membranes- AKA the gums- look at the area under the lip and above the teeth- what color is it?

Normal: pink
Not Normal: pale pink, cherry red, bluish, yellow

Capillary refill time (CRT) – is completed by lifting the upper lip, pressing the gum above the teeth to make the gum pale and measuring how long it takes to return back to pink. 1-2 seconds is normal

Heart/Lungs- listen for breathing and feel the heart by placing a hand along the side of the cat's chest or placing a hand on the inside of the cat's back leg

Normal: regular heart rate and easy breathing, even moving of the chest in and out with breathing
Not Normal: any noises heard as cat breaths, irregular, slow or fast heart rate, coughing, any visible signs of difficulty breathing- such as opening the mouth to breathe, any blue coloring of the mouth, if the cat is unable to rest or lie down

Abdomen- feel the abdomen of the cat by placing your hands just behind the ribs and gently pressing into the abdomen – move slowly and gently from the front of the abdomen to the back of the abdomen

Normal: soft, not painful, slim (if the pet is not overweight), no lumps, bumps, masses
Not normal: large, tense, rounded, painful when touching, any lumps, bumps, or masses

Neurological– exam the pet's ability to walk properly and respond properly

Normal: the cat can feel you touch them; all four paws stand properly on the floor, able to walk in a straight line
Not Normal: head tilting to one side, inability to walk, pain or no pain when pinching paws, seizures, fainting, inability to wake a pet, paws knuckling over

Skin/Coat-look at and feel the pet's skin and hair coat

Normal: shiny, smooth, soft, unbroken hair and smooth skin, minimal odor
Not Normal: sparse or patchy hair coat, open sores or wounds, growths, excess oil in the skin, dry skin, reddening, odor, rash

Extremities- look at all 4 legs of the pet

Normal: able to walk evenly on all 4 legs, no deformities, no growths, no swelling,
Not Normal: unable to walk on 1 or more legs, swelling, pain when touching areas, growths, dangling legs, open wounds, odor, discharge of any color

Lymph nodes- these may be difficult to locate on a cat unless they are enlarged.

Normal: unable to feel lymph nodes
Not Normal: swelling in the areas of the lymph nodes- under the jaw, in front of the front legs, in front of the back legs, behind the knees, in the groin or under the front legs

Muscles and bones- look at the cat's back and legs and muscles over the body

Normal: muscles soft and covering the bones evenly on both sides of the body part being examined, able to walk without pain,
Not Normal: small muscle size in any area, tense muscles, pain when gently feeling over the spine and other body areas, pain when walking, jumping, or playing

Urogenital- exam the cat's ability to pass urine and the male and female parts of the cat

Normal: clean and dry areas- no discharge, swelling, pain
Not Normal: any licking of the areas, swelling, discharge, odor, inability to urinate – this may be difficult if a large amount of litter is in the box because cats sometimes appear to be urinating and are not – the inability to urinate is an emergency

Perineum- examine the area under the tail area

Normal: clean and dry, no swelling
Not Normal: swelling, discharge, odor, scooting, licking

Tail– examine the pet's tail

Normal: able to hold tail upright, able to move the tail
Not Normal: inability to move tail, growths, swelling, pain, crooked tail, open wounds

Feet – examine the cat's feet and nails

Normal: nails are an appropriate length and clean and dry, no swelling to any areas of the paws, warm to the touch
Not Normal: swelling in any digit or area of the paw, discharge from any area of the paw, thick, discolored nails, curvature of the nails into the paw pads, discharge from the nail beds

SENIOR PETS

Our cats are loyal for many years. With improved veterinary care, they are living longer lives.

When is a cat considered a senior pet? Most consider cats to be seniors when they are over 10 years of age.

As cats age, age related conditions discussed in prior chapters arise and include:

- arthritis – cats may be painful and less active
- dental disease – can be found as early as 1-3 years of age, however, worsens with aging
- thyroid disease – usually a disorder where too much thyroid hormone is being made by the cat's thyroid gland
- thyroid disease can lead to high blood pressure in senior cats
- kidney disease – a very common condition in cats
- increased urination – which may be from kidney, thyroid, or other disorders
- liver disease
- urinary disease
- weight changes – may lose weight if not eating well due to arthritis pain or dental disease – or overweight due to less activity
- weakness – from disease or arthritis
- the cat's immune system may be less able to fight off infection/disease
- dehydration may be a consequence of many disease processes that occur in cats
- fragile skin – easily injured or infected
- decreased grooming – cats may needs matted hair removed by a veterinarian or groomer, increased brushing, and treatment for resulting skin irritation
- the claws of older cats are sometimes thicker, overgrown, and brittle
- senility – as noted if the cat wanders, meows excessively, is obviously disoriented to the owner or surroundings, or may avoid social interaction
- decreased appetite – may be due to discomfort, disease, or even decreased ability to smell the food being eaten

(Continued disorders in aging cats)

- behavior changes may occur – cats that are aging may become more fearful of circumstances around them or more aggressive in certain situations – whether pain or disorientation initiates this change
- diabetes
- heart disease
- cancer
- vision and hearing loss

Signs that may be observed in our senior cats include:

- signs of pain when getting up from resting
- difficulty going up and down steps
- increase in the times they urinate/defecate
- soiling in the house when did not before – being unable to get to or in and out of the litter box
- confusion
- sleeping more
- exaggerated reactions to sounds
- bumping into objects
- not hearing being called or sensing danger outside
- an increase in anxiety
- a decrease in the ability to keep themselves clean
- repetitive activity
- wandering
- an increase in the chance of skin growths and other cancers
- loss of appetite

Goals for Senior Cats include:

- providing the healthiest and highest quality of life
- reduce factors that may lead to health risks
- detect disorders/disease as early and quickly as possible
- correct or delay the progression of any disease as much as possible
- improve and maintain the health of the cat in general

What we can do for our senior cats includes:

- close observation – note any changes as they occur
- watch their physical activity – exercise them as able – for their muscle strength, weight management and overall health
- make food and water easily accessible
- provide senior nutrition to avoid weight loss or weight gain – ask your veterinarian to recommend a diet for your cat's age and medical needs
- keep the litter box in a convenient area for the cat- may need lower sides to make it more comfortable to climb in and out of
- keep their environment fun for them – play with them and allow them to exercise as they are able
- avoid drastic changes in their environment – change is stressful to senior cats
- monitor urine production
- monitor bowel movements- constipation requires treatment
- keep as active as they are able without overdoing it
- medicate if in pain/discomfort
- consider their dietary needs as they age
- observe their eating habits
- visit the veterinarian at least twice a year – testing and exams can help detect disorders early
- treat conditions that develop as soon as possible
- consider routine blood work to identify disorders early
- senior proof your home- watch for furniture that may cause harm if bumped into, close off stairs, use ramps, make food and water bowls accessible
- be aware of vision or hearing loss
- monitor the pet's dental health and brush and care for their teeth daily
- brush their coat daily – with disorders of aging or saliva changes in the aging cat or pain from arthritis, some cats do not groom themselves well

(Continued things we can do for our senior cats)

- trim their nails often
- protect the senior pets from temperature changes
- use soft blankets for comfort
- use rugs and carpeted areas for ease of walking and rising as needed
- never assume changes in a cat's behavior is just 'due to older age' and not treatable, there are many available treatments to help cats live healthy and longer lives
- have your cat visit the veterinarian at least twice a year and whenever you have a concern
- cherish every moment – time goes very fast when we love our cats

BRUSHING

All cats – including senior cats- benefit from brushing regularly-

Many cats loved being brushed. While important for all cats, brushing is very important for long haired cats. Brushing:
- removes loose hairs- this decreases the amount of hair swallowed by the cat- which helps decrease hair balls from forming
- stimulates blood circulation and oil gland production- this makes the skin and hair coat shinier and healthier
- encourages owners to observe their cat's skin and hair coat as well as their nails – which may need to be clipped – especially in older cats

Starting brushing cats when they are kittens is helpful for successful positive experience with and response to brushing.

Many recommend short haired be brushed at least weekly and long haired cats daily.

BATHING

Without a doubt, bathing cats can be an owner's greatest challenge.

While most cats groom themselves, there may be times bathing is recommended.

My suggestion is that if you are an owner who would like to bath your cat, or thinks you may need to at some time; you may want to consider starting them in the tub or sink when they are wee little kittens. This gets them used to the water.

When introducing bathing to a kitten or cat, you may consider starting with a warm wet washcloth or sponge. If they react negatively, talk in a soothing voice to reassure the kitten or cat it is ok.

When you want to introduce a kitten or cat to a full bath, I recommend placing them in a tub or sink with warm – but not HOT water (96-98 degrees) – by gently submerging their bodies into the water, allowing them time to adjust to being all wet. If you are able, remove them from the water, lather them in 'cat safe' shampoo, then rinse them well by either submerging them again or using a hose/sprayer with a gentle spray, and drying them well – using a hair dryer if needed.

WHILE NOT COMPLETELY SCIENTIFIC, APPROXIMATE AGES OF CATS COMPARED TO HUMAN YEARS ARE:

CAT	HUMAN
0-1 Month	0-1 year
2-3 months	2-4 years
4 months	6-8 years
6 months	10 years
7 months	12 years
12 months	15-16 years
18 months	21 years
2 years	23-24 years
3 years	28 years
4 years	32 years

And 4 years of human years for each year of cat years from 5 and older.

CATS ARE CONSIDERED…..

Kittens – from birth to 6 months of age

Juniors – from 7 months – 2 years of age

Prime age- from 3- 6 years of age

Mature- from 7-10 years of age

Seniors- from 11-14 years of age

Geriatric – over 15 years of age

THE END

This is so long for now, but it is really never the end. There is always more to learn and share.

www.ingramcontent.com/pod-product-compliance
Lightning Source LLC
Chambersburg PA
CBHW050858240426
43673CB00009B/281